Foreword by Anthony C. Sciré
Author of *The Power of 2*

LIVING WITHOUT LIMITS

Say "Yes!" to "How?" and
Break Through to a Life Filled
with Infinite Possibilities

JACK SMITH

A ***Possibility Press*** Book

LIVING WITHOUT LIMITS

Say "Yes!" to "How?" and
Break Through to a Life Filled
with Infinite Possibilities

Jack Smith

Foreword by Anthony C. Sciré
Artwork by Mike Schuler

Published by
Possibility Press
info@possibilitypress.com

Manufactured in the United States of America

Dedication

To my beloved wife, Vickey, who introduced me to my faith
and a life filled with limitless possibilities.

Acknowledgment

My dream of becoming an author has been a journey filled
with encouragement and love, given endlessly and unsel-
fishly by my friends and family. For that, and much
more, I will remain forever grateful. My wife and two daughters
have shared and supported my every endeavor. They taught me that
success isn't about position; it's about passion.

One of my best friends, Mike Schuler, graciously took the time to
create the pictures for this book. He's as genuine in life and spirit as
anyone I've ever met. His honesty, warmth, compassion, and concern shine for everyone to see. He has shown me that the answer to
"How?" is always "Yes!" With friends like him, how could I not be
encouraged to reach for the stars? He is more than a friend; he is a
brother in Christ who motivated me to know the difference between
the tire kickers and the buyers. There are those who live their lives
tip-toeing around what they really want, but then there are those who
pay the price for the ride of their lives.

Thank you to the staff at Possibility Press who worked hard to
help make this book what it is. For that and the friendship we've developed, I am deeply grateful.

Last, but certainly not least, thank you God for, without you, none
of this would have been possible.

Jack Smith

Contents

Do Good, Have Fun,
and Make Money!

*"Are you ready to break through the limits you've
accepted in the past, to reach the pinnacle of whatever you are
passionate about claiming?"*
—Tony Sciré—

Wow! What an honor and great pleasure it is to write the foreword for *Living Without Limits*. The book is especially relevant for me, as I recently made the big break from the limits of corporate life to being on my own. It's great and I love it!

Now don't get me wrong, I had a great ride for many years with MCI and was able to climb the success ladder to vice president of International Relations/Europe. But the ladder was not leaning against the wall of my passion—speaking and writing. It was leaning against the wrong wall.

Jack, a man of great accomplishment, although he's too humble to admit it, has had a lot of people setting limits for him which he had to overcome. So he has quite a story to tell. With this book, he can help you get a new perspective on how you can get free of whatever self- or other-imposed limits you may have accepted that are holding you back. Jack's writing makes you feel as if you are sitting in his living room being mentored by a man with experience

5

and a sense of humor that will make you smile and even laugh out loud. Not many can spin a tale to get a life-changing point across like Jack can.

One of my mottos is "Do good, have fun, and make money!" When you continue to do good for others in your business or career and have fun with it, the money will come. I've lived a great life so far, and have had a great corporate run, but it took me twenty-eight years to follow Jack's advice to live a really powerful life without limits. I only wish I had taken his advice years ago.

Are you one of those people who has an opportunity right in front of you to do exactly that? Are you ready to break through the limits you've accepted in the past, to reach the pinnacle of whatever success you are passionate about claiming? I hope so. It's the only way you can really discover what you're made of and the only way you can create a great life for yourself.

Read this extraordinary book, live without limits, and make it happen—*for you!*

Blessings "2" you,

Tony Sciré
Speaker, Consultant, and Author of *The Power of 2*

"*When you are inspired by some great purpose, some extraordinary project, all of your thoughts break their bonds. Your mind transcends limitations. Your consciousness expands in every direction and you find yourself in a new, great, and wonderful world. Dormant forces that weren't accessible to you and facilities and talents come alive, and you discover yourself to be a greater person, by far, than you ever dreamed yourself to be.*"

—Patangali

"*The limits people set for themselves or accept from others form the dimensions of their reality. Will you spend your entire life talking about what you could, would, or should have done yesterday or will do tomorrow—or seize the opportunity and power of the moment?*"

—Jack Smith

Is Your Foot on the Brake or the Accelerator?

"It's up to you to stand your ground and clearly claim your dream."
—Jack Smith—

For years, I let manuscripts lie around the office or sit trapped in the computer. I never went for my dream because I let fear keep me stuck in neutral. The dream engine was revving alright, but my thoughts of failure and rejection caused me to set a limit that wouldn't allow me to put it in drive and hit the accelerator. My wonderful wife, Vickey, had been telling me for years to just go for it, but my foot had been planted firmly on the brake.

If I were a bird, I would've been content to swing on the perch in my cage. Even though the door of opportunity was wide open, I would've just sat there and swung back and forth in my "air rut"— doing nothing.

I encourage you to shed any limits others are imposing on you and any you are, perhaps unwittingly, hanging onto from the past. I urge you to shed the shackles you may be in and head for the mountaintop of life. The foundation is a strong work ethic, and the draw is a worthwhile goal or dream. But how does one break through the limits and stay excited enough to keep going? And what about those who say you can't do it?

Over the years, I've used the principles, thoughts, and ideas in this book and shared them with many people. I wish I could say everyone took my advice. Then they, too, could have discovered how rewarding and exciting it can be to set your sights on something special—and then go for it.

The limits people set for themselves or accept from others form the dimensions of their reality. Will you spend your entire life talking about what you could, would, or should have done yesterday or will do tomorrow—or seize the opportunity and power of the moment? Have you ever wondered what happened to the twenty-four hours you have every day? I used to, but I don't anymore.

There were two things that helped kick me into action: 1) a friend named Mike who believed in me, and 2) the realization that the only permission I needed to go forward was from me!

I hope this book inspires you to never allow yourself or anyone else set your limits. Many will try to throw up roadblocks, but you'll keep going. They'll fail to stop you because you've become a no-limit person. Ideally, they'll have a change of heart and join you! Had I listened to the critics who had never written anything for publication, you wouldn't be reading this book.

Continue dreaming and reaching for the life you envision. Who is to be more admired; the person who reaches for his or her dream or the one who sets or accepts limits and refuses to take action?

To Your Success,

Jack Smith

"**A**rgue *for
your limita-
tions and,
sure enough,
they're
yours.*"

—Richard Bach

"Twenty years from now you will be more disappointed by the things you didn't do than by the things you did do. So throw off the bowlines. Sail away from safe harbor. Catch the trade winds in your sails. Explore. Dream. Discover."

—Mark Twain

—Chapter One—

What to Do if *"They"* Say You Can't

"Always stay on track!"
—Jack Smith—

As a wise person once said, "Worrying is like a rocking chair. It gives you something to do but you don't get very far." Others can set our limits only if we give them permission to do so. Have you ever allowed anyone to set yours? If so, what you're about to read will encourage you to tune them out. Before you know it, you'll be breaking the bonds of your limits and shining with all the potential within you.

After serving his tour of duty within the U.S. Marines, a young man met the woman of his dreams. After a four-month courtship, the couple made their marriage vows in a preacher's home with only five present, including the bride and groom. Ten months later, they were blessed with their first child. Being a very faith-filled couple, they agreed he would go into the ministry. This would mean hard work and extensive study at one of the finest universities. Could he do it? His friends and family said no; his wife smiled and said yes.

He had graduated forty-seventh in a high school class of fifty-three, and had never applied himself to anything except sports. Many had given up on him and certainly not without reason. He had spent three years getting through his senior course requirements and had four warrants out for his arrest when he joined the Marines. But he also had one deep-down gnawing desire that drove him. The oldest son of his family, he earnestly desired to be a better husband and father than his dad was. His father not only tried to set limits for him, but did it in a cruel-hearted way, hurling such comments at him as, "You'll never amount to anything"; "You're just stupid"; "You'll never have anything." It's sad that some people never get beyond the limits they permitted an unkind person to set for them—perhaps a parent, teacher, peer, or someone else. Fortunately, others seek and obtain the help they need from positive supportive friends like mentors or leaders.

The Challenge to Succeed

This was the big day. There he sat in front of a big desk, in his new clothes with a fresh haircut, waiting for the professor to come in and welcome him to the university. At least, that's what he assumed this meeting was to be about. Entering the room in a handsome navy suit, the professor seemed friendly enough. His expression was quite serious and he wore his glasses low on his nose, giving him a distinctly intellectual look. "Young man," the professor began, "I've been going over your high school transcript." "Yes, sir," replied the former Marine. "Well, to put it bluntly, I'm not sure you're college material," the professor confessed. "Why would you say that?" the young man inquired, looking puzzled. "Well," the professor continued, "with your low grades, I don't want to waste your time nor ours."

Now the young man began feeling sick and numb. Here was someone else besides his father trying to set his limits! The prospective student envisioned a bull's-eye in the middle of the professor's forehead. My, did he ever want to tell him *exactly* what he was thinking! Nevertheless, he continued showing respect for the gentleman who was obviously in charge.

Do You Believe You Can?

"Sir, are you asking me to take my wife and small child and go home?" the younger man asked. "No," the older man responded,

"What I *am* telling you, though, is that we're reluctantly letting you into the university, even though we're sure you can't possibly make it." Devastated, the young man went home and cried for hours. His wife did her best to console him. Later, after he'd calmed down, she looked at him and said something that gave him the incentive to do his best: "Honey, I had a teacher one time who always ended every class with something Henry Ford said that I'll never forget. 'Whether you believe you can or whether you believe you can't, you're right.'" He took that as a challenge to believe he could!

It's All About Work Ethic—*and Not Accepting Any Limits*

At the end of the new student's first semester, the professor, once again, called him into his office. "Yes, sir, you wanted to see me?" the young man asked. Smiling, the professor said, "You are our most pleasant surprise! You made two As and two Bs, a 3.5 GPA (Grade Point Average). You've really worked hard and shown that you have what it takes to be a success." With tears welling up in his eyes, the pupil responded, "Thank you, sir. Coming from you, that means more to me than you'll ever know." "Young man," the professor continued, "there are two things I want to tell you. First of all, you've learned a very important lesson—that a strong work ethic is essential for success. It's not that you have one set of ethics for home, another with friends, and yet another for work. It's that when you live life by the finest ethics, there is no need to differentiate—they permeate every aspect of your life. The consistency of always doing your best to do the right thing will elevate you above the standards of the world."

The student smiled, shook the professor's outstretched hand, and confidently said, "Thank you so much for letting me be a part of this university."

"That brings me to the second thing I wanted to tell you," responded the professor, adjusting his glasses. "Remember, in our first meeting, when I said we were letting you in but that you probably wouldn't make it?" "Yes," replied the student with a sigh. "Well," the older man continued, "the only reason I told you that was to prod you into either digging down to do the work or quitting and going back home. Thank you for working so hard to accomplish your dream."

The young man went on to graduate and has been preaching full-time for many years. As you might have guessed, I was that young man!

She Decided What She Could Do—*No One Else!*

One of my favorite athletes of all time is Mary Lou Retton. This petite package of competitive dynamite stood up against adversity and walked away an Olympic champion. Nothing was going to keep her from giving her dream her best shot. Because of this determination, she was named *Sports Illustrated* magazine's "Sportswoman of the Year" in 1984.

Success for Mary Lou, as with many seeking to achieve, didn't come without its dues. Just six weeks before the Olympic games were to begin, her doctors told her that she wouldn't be able to compete. She needed knee surgery right away. It appeared that all her work studying dance and acrobatics since age four, and gymnastics starting at five, had been for naught.

Mary Lou went ahead and had the surgery and did the necessary rehabilitation in time to compete, and compete she did. At sixteen, and coming off serious knee surgery, the odds of performing a great jump, let alone a perfect one, were almost nil. Ekaterina Szabo was leading Mary Lou by .05 of a point. Using her speed and power, Mary Lou exploded down the runway and nailed her attempt on the vault for a perfect 10. She not only became the first woman to win an individual Olympic medal in gymnastics, but she also led her USA team to win a silver.

She went on to win three more individual medals. Mary Lou refused to say no to her dream—to let anyone else decide what she could do. When the doctors told her she couldn't, Mary Lou said, "I've made it this far. No one's going to keep me from trying." She knew the answer to "How?" was "Yes!" A full decade after her victories, an Associated Press national survey named Mary Lou Retton the "Most Popular Athlete in America." Not bad for someone who dared to dream big dreams and wouldn't take no for an answer!

There will always be those who try to set our limits—they think they know us better than we know ourselves. It's that way in business, religion, community, family life, and everywhere else. Why would we want to accept the limits others may thrust on us—especially by those who fail to dream and stretch beyond where *they* are?

We were all created to become the best we can be. What we become is the result of the choices we make and the actions we take. Boldly announce: "I never give permission for anyone else to set limits as to what I can or can't accomplish!"

The Three Rules of Success

Remember the following three rules of success, regardless of what limits you may have accepted from yourself in the past or the limits others may have tried to impose on you. Are you ready for them? Here they are:

Rule 1: Stay on track!
Rule 2: Stay on track!
Rule 3: Stay on track!

If you get sidetracked, you've set limits on yourself and your potential to achieve what you desire!

"*Has your comfort or familiar zone become your limit? Why might you have chosen to never extend beyond where you are today? How long will you watch others fulfill their dreams while not fulfilling your own?*"

—Jack Smith

Chapter Two

Going Beyond the Limits of Your "Comfort" Zone

"If you don't go after what you want, you'll never have it. If you don't step forward, you're always in the same place."
—Jack Smith—

Many never get started building a future because doing so would mean climbing out of the limits of their so-called comfort zone. All of us have such a zone or, perhaps, several of them. They are places where we stay or return, mentally or physically, in an often-futile attempt to avoid changes or challenges. They probably aren't even all that comfortable, just familiar! The door of opportunity may stand wide open, but, like birds in a cage, we stay on our perch, consume the same food and drink, associate with the same cage partners, and sing the same tune. The freedom for achieving a better life is just outside our cage, but there we habitually sit. We're swinging close to the limits the cage imposes, and our belly is full, but we're still in the cage.

Trapped in a Cage

As the couple drove up to the gas pump, they simply couldn't believe what they saw—a twelve-by-twelve-foot cage, filthy inside, with cans, bottles, and candy wrappers strewn everywhere. The bucket of dirty brown water had obviously been in there for quite a while. The black bear locked inside looked miserable as he paced back and forth—bored within the confines of his prison.

Having seen as much as they could tolerate, the couple went into the ramshackle little store. They wanted to talk to the bedraggled gas station owner to see if he was interested in selling the bear. As they talked, they glanced outside and noticed that some kids were poking at the bear with a stick, trying to make him angry enough to growl. The couple agreed to buy the bear for the asking price, and planned to come back in a few days to take him to his new home.

Shifting Out of Neutral—*Put It in Gear*

Upon returning to the gas station, the man and his wife lovingly loaded the docile caged bear onto a truck. They had decided to take him to a friend's place who not only kept bears but also a variety of other animals as well. The couple was confident that their new furry friend would be well cared for. Upon arrival, they gently unloaded the cage inside the new compound where the bear would reside for the remainder of his life. The compound was many times larger and certainly much cleaner than his old home. The water trough was filled with an abundance of clear, fresh water. In one corner was more food than the bear saw in a week from his previous owner.

The desireability of the transfer from filth to the sublime would be obvious, even for a bear, wouldn't you agree? Wrong! The door to the cage was opened and nothing happened. The bear didn't budge an inch! It had to be encouraged in soothing tones and eventually prodded to leave the cage. After the big fellow finally ventured out, he just moved around in a twelve-foot square. Astounded, the new owners were so disappointed they felt sick to their stomachs. The bear's internal limits had been strongly set. His mind had been in neutral for so long that whatever potential he had to freely roam about was long forgotten. He had been "melted" into someone else's mold and had learned to survive within those constraints. But as unhappy as he was, he never made his protests known nor even tried to break loose.

Don't Be a Branch Sitter—*Go Out on a Limb*

How *do* we muster the courage to step out of our so-called comfort zone? The courage to stretch and do something new—accomplish a dream or goal that's important to us—comes with believing in ourselves. In some cases, this belief is born and then nurtured by a supportive, caring network of friends who believe in us and our capability to achieve what we desire to accomplish. If this is the case for you, treasure those friends and drink up the support like a thirsty wanderer who crosses a desert and finds a well on the other side. The belief that we can make it happen fuels our desire to make the thought a reality. The reverse of this is also true—either way, our desire fuels our belief! If it's strong enough, our desire drives us to take all the necessary steps and never give up in our quest.

So why aren't *more* people successful? They slip into the habits and melt into the mold (like the bear did) of their current job, reinforcing the characteristics required to endure it. Usually, whatever they may say they aspire to beyond that is just talk. You can easily talk about doing something outside of your job or about believing in yourself and going beyond any limits you may have accepted in the past. But, as they say, "Talk is cheap!" You haven't really accomplished anything until you release your grip on the tree trunk of old habits. Stop being a branch sitter. Leave your comfort zone and go out on a limb. Take risks to achieve freedom and success, or whatever your goal may be. Ah, there's the first hurdle to overcome in any new endeavor. "Did you say, *limb*?" Yes, leaving any comfort zone is to travel in new territory. That's exciting!

See in Three "D"—*Dream, Discuss, and Deliver*

"My," some say, "that sounds *so* daring!" There are three "Ds" we can take from the word DARE which, when teamed together, create success. As we dare, we need to Dream, Discuss, and Deliver. First, we'll discuss the dream.

Dream, the first "D," is easy. All of us have dreams—even if we've ignored them for so long we've almost forgotten them. All of us, at one time or another, have imagined ourselves as the most beautiful or handsome, the best athlete, a famous rock or movie star, a millionaire, or something else. So take a piece of paper and write down your dream and all of its components—the bigger your list the better. Be a multiple-dream person. Don't pity one-dream people, especially those who haven't yet accomplished it. Encourage and help them make it come true.

Many people envision going from where they are to where they want to be and stop—never surging ahead and doing what it takes to get from point A to point Z. Whatever your biggest dream is, start to make it real by reprioritizing your life and doing the required work to reach it. Sad to say, but for many, it's their unwillingness to do this that keeps them from going beyond their limits. Be one of those daring souls who embraces risk and overcomes obstacles. Striving for your dreams makes life a grand adventure.

Discuss, the second "D," is essential. Discuss your dream with a supportive person who is already successful or with someone who can connect you with such a person. This is essential. Surround yourself with those who believe in your dream. There will always be the Negative Nellies—those who put you and your dream down. They tell you it can't be done, or if it could, it wouldn't be by you.

Have you ever gone to an atheist for spiritual advice or to an attorney for medical advice? Why would anyone even consider going to someone who is afraid and confined to his or her own limits for advice about getting out of theirs? Always remember that the people around us will probably do one of four "I" things—indict, ignore, indulge, or inspire us. Choose to associate with those who inspire you to push beyond your so-called limits.

Deliver, the third "D," is the most important. Deliver on what you have dreamed and discussed. All the talk and wishful thinking in the world won't make it happen if we don't take the appropriate steps to go from where we are to where we want to be. This is the point when the fear of failure may whisper in your ear and tell you how silly your dreams are. It shouts that you will be battered and bruised by all the pitfalls dream seeking seems to bring.

It isn't the size of the challenges we encounter on the way to our dreams that matter. It's the attitude that we'll overcome whatever comes our way—translated into action—that wins the day. It isn't encountering roadblocks that constitutes failure. It's never overcoming them that's so sad.

Extending Beyond Yourself

Has your comfort or familiar zone become your limit? Why might you have chosen to never extend beyond where you are today? How long will you watch others fulfill their dreams, while not fulfilling your own?"

Everyone is capable of more success. Believe in yourself and your dreams, and associate with encouragers rather than discouragers. Break through and go beyond your limits.

"**L**ots of people have the 'want to,' but never reach that 'one day' when they step out of where they are and into the field of possibilities. They automatically lose rather than seize the chance to win."

—Jack Smith

Chapter Three

How Do You Get Started?

"It's time to go for it!"
—Jack Smith—

My dream since college, in addition to my preaching, was to write. So I asked a man who was successfully doing both for some much-needed mentoring on how to get started.

He leaned back in his stuffed leather chair, smiled, and said, "What did you do before you became a preacher?"

"Well, sir," I said, "I worked in a manufacturing plant in a small town in Arkansas."

"How did you get started there?" he asked.

Puzzled, I said, "I don't understand what you're asking."

He responded, "Jack, what I mean is how did you get started at that job?"

That "One-Day" Thing

Was this kind gentleman asking me some kind of a trick question?

"Well, one day I went…."

"Excuse me," he immediately interrupted, "what was that you just said?"

"I said, one day…."

He interrupted me again, "So did I!"

"So did you *what*?" I asked.

"You know, that one-day thing?" he smiled. "I did that too!"

Then it finally dawned on me. What he was saying was that in everything we pursue, including our dreams and goals, we always get started in the same way—"one day."

No one gets started by passing up that one day! This is the day when all the talk and preparation is finally over and you start *doing* it. This may sound silly but it's the honest truth. Lots of people have the "want-to," but never reach that one day when they step out of where they are and into the field of possibilities. They automatically lose rather than seize the chance to win. Consider the following example...

More Talented Than We Thought

This boy had always been withdrawn and shy. In fact, we'd almost never notice him around school unless his name was called in class. He was that one kid who seems to be in every grade; the one who's shunned and made fun of because of some supposed abnormality. He didn't fit in and he knew it; he even seemed to accept it as his fate.

Being poor and having one of the worst cases of acne didn't help his self-esteem either. All any of us knew about this fella was that he'd ride the bus back and forth to school, going straight home after classes. He was never seen at any school functions. This kid never attended any sporting events, nor went out for any team. You wouldn't even see him around the town square on Saturdays or at special town events. None of us could ever remember him being in the downtown theater or at Dog and Sud's Drive-In, where practically everyone went at one time or another.

Then came that one day in this kid's life. It was time for the yearly talent show. Several acts were listed, including mine; I played guitar in a band. All the talk before the competition, though, was about that one reclusive student. Amazingly, he had signed up to perform—whatever his talent was! Only the names were mentioned—not the respective talents. People just laughed at the mention of anything this young, quiet, unpopular boy could possibly do.

When his name was announced, the audience fell into an immediate hush....

The talent show was being held in the downtown theater and was considered a very big event. After all, the winner would be taking home a trophy and cash. But the idea of this shy kid competing was so inconceivable that I personally thought there must have been some mistake—that even though his name was called, it had to have been a misprint. Surely, a different person would have walked out to perform. But no, by goodness, it was *really* the shy kid that appeared! He slowly walked across the stage with his head down, obviously fearing eye contact.

What was he going to do? Sit down and play the piano? Yes, that's exactly where he was headed. I chuckled inside thinking, "I wonder how many verses of the 'Mary Had a Little Lamb' nursery rhyme he knows!" Once seated, he pulled the microphone closer and smiled. Looking out into the audience, he said, "If Jerry Lee Lewis were here tonight, this is what he would sound like."

Now, friends, let me tell you, he almost wore that piano out! It was the most amazing transformation any of us had ever seen. What we didn't know was that his momma taught piano, and it was her prize student who was now on stage wowing the entire student body.

He was as good as anyone I'd ever heard—then or since. Not only did he win the contest, he also had several standing ovations and requests. He played every single song easily and beautifully. We all looked at him and thought, "No way!" We couldn't believe it! He had shown us that he'd been diligently preparing for *his* one day.

Once Just a Young Girl with a Dream

Born November 14, 1954 in Birmingham, Alabama, Condoleeza Rice would, 51 years later, be named "the world's most powerful woman" by *Forbes* magazine. When her father told her that she could become President of the United States, African Americans didn't yet even have the right to vote. With a name derived from an Italian musical term meaning "tender mercies," Condoleeza is living proof that a will to achieve, breaking through limits, and hard work are prerequisites for success.

She was playing the piano by age three and became an excellent reader by five. In an article on her life, the author said Condoleeza would wake up at 4:30 a.m. to exercise and then play music. She let nothing, not even racial barriers, stand in her way. She entered the University of Denver at 15 and graduated at 19, with a Bachelors degree in Political Science. In 1975, she received a Masters degree from Notre Dame, and, in 1981, a Doctorate from the University of Denver.

Speaking fluent Russian, Condoleeza defended her dissertation on the relations between Russia and Czechoslovakia, and later wrote a book about it. She speaks five languages and holds honorary Doctorates from Moorehouse College, the University of Alabama, Notre Dame, National Defense University, Mississippi College School of Law, the University of Louisville, and Michigan State University.

In 1999, she completed a six-year tenure as Stanford University's Provost. As Chief Budget and Academics Officer, Dr. Rice was the one responsible for a $1.5 billion annual budget. This program involved 1,400 faculty members and 14,000 students. In addition to that, she was also a corporate board member of Chevron, the Hewlett Foundation, and Charles Schwab. You can see that this marvelous woman could never be convinced of any limits. She now travels the world as Madame Secretary. Dr. Condoleeza Rice, Secretary of State, scholar, and woman of vision and dedication, was, at one time, just a young girl with a dream.

The Courage to Face the Critics

So how do *you* get started? First, you decide to do so. Then you muster up your courage in the face of even the toughest critics, and dare to deliver your best performance in spite of any fear you may have. Even if others are making judgments about you and what you're doing or proposing to do, you know deep in your heart what you've got a hold of and what you need to do to make it happen. It's putting that together with a strong desire to give your best performance that gets you started. Finally, it's coming to that *one day* when there's no turning back. It's time to go for it. It's as if you've signed up for this special day. Your name is called and you walk across life's stage and give it your all.

What about the outcome? You'll never begin to know until you reach that one day when there is no turning back. Financial independence, personal freedom, or whatever your dream or goal is will only come after you win the war. What war? The war with self-imposed limits and those who are against your idea. Remember, as someone wise said, "There are no statues erected to critics!"

"Doubt sees the obstacles, Faith sees the way. Doubt sees the dark of night, Faith sees the day. Doubt dreads to take a step, but Faith soars on high. Doubt questions, who believes? Faith answers I."

—Rich DeVos

Chapter Four

The Answer to "How?" Is "Yes!"

"Make things happen to feed your dream or it will starve to death."
—Jack Smith—

My life story has been filled with challenges, discouragement, abuse, and embarrassment. My mother was the best; my father the worst. At an early age, I listened to and unknowingly allowed others to "drive a stake into my heart," taking away my ability to care or even try to excel. They judged me according to what they had seen in my father. He was the town drunk and a professional gambler; hardly something in a town of 3,500 that could be kept secret, especially when the county, at that time, was dry!

I watched my father abuse my mother, even long after they divorced when I was twelve. At fourteen, I was basically on my own living in Mountain Home, Arkansas. I stayed with Dad to finish my freshman year of high school and play football—not the wisest decision I ever made. He was out much of the time with his friends, leaving me to fend for myself or perish! My dad did do one thing for me during this time, besides, of course, teaching me what not to do. He paid two months rent in advance for a ten-by-forty-foot trailer located on a dark dirt road about five miles outside of town. During all this, I was just too embarrassed to ask for help.

Survival—*the First Order of Business*

I was going to school by bus in the morning and walking home in the evenings. On this particular occasion, I hadn't eaten in a couple of days when it finally dawned on me that right across the fence, behind the trailer, was the proverbial pot of gold. Apples! Green, shiny, round apples, all I could eat. So what if there was a "No Trespassing" sign or two nailed to the fence? I was hungry. The electricity and water had been turned off a week earlier, and all I had to drink was the water from melted ice in the freezer trays. It tasted "fuzzy" but it was great at the time.

I hurled my burly 133-pound body over that fence, past the "No Trespassing" signs and up that tree. All that weekend, I ate green apples and sipped fuzzy water. I *could* survive after all. It was here that I learned the answer to "How?" is "Yes!" I would never advocate breaking any laws, but, while sitting in that tree, something became abundantly clear. All those classmates who told me I was worthless, poor, and would never amount to anything were really telling me not to trespass on their lives. No one else cared as much as I did about how, or even whether, I survived.

With that in mind, I got a job at a local restaurant for the grand wage of fifty cents an hour. I worked four hours a night. Wow, I made two dollars a night; I was a rich young man! I could order whatever I wanted off the menu—as long as I paid for it. It was obviously time to adapt and overcome, since I wasn't about to make two dollars and then give most of it back for a cheeseburger, fries, and Coke supper. So, I came up with a plan.

I put a paper sack under the sink and whenever plates came into the kitchen with chicken, shrimp, or steak that looked like it hadn't been touched, it went into the bag. How many kids do you know that ate like that for supper and breakfast? Again, the answer to "How?" is "Yes!" Make things happen to feed your dream or it will starve to death.

During the summer when I was sixteen, I lived in a tent on a river bank in Smyrna, Tennessee. I was there to work, pulling cable behind a bulldozer, getting things ready for creating a man-made lake. My best friend and I lived on potatoes and pork and beans. That was one of the hottest, longest, and most unpleasant summers of my life. It was also scary for us, two boys on our own, when people and animals visited our campsite all hours of the night. What were we thinking? But, as bad as it was, it was still a welcome relief to be away from my father. He had attempted suicide right in front of his sons, tried to set the house on fire with us in it, broke my mother's nose, ribs, and fingers, and many times beat us with his fists.

A Glimmer of Improvement

Jumping forward a couple years, it is 1968 and I am in my *third* year as a senior. That's right, you are reading a book written by someone who spent six years in high school! I graduated in May 1969 and turned twenty in July. It was a caring stepfather who reminded me that the answer to "How?" was "Yes!" He also told me that, even if he never did anything else for me, he was going to see to it that I got a high school diploma which, of course, I did. He wouldn't allow me to just quit.

So, here we were, in Maize, Kansas, just outside of Wichita, living in a one-room garage covered on the outside with black tar paper and on the inside with bags of exposed insulation. We divided the one room into three rooms with cut-up pieces of cardboard refrigerator cartons. We were still poor but it was a new start with a new man giving me direction. The kids at school no longer looked down on us. In fact, they thought it was "far-out" that we had no running water, just a pump in the sink. We also had the luxury of choosing which side we wanted to use in our two-seater outhouse.

Building Better Tomorrows

My brother and I helped our stepfather build that garage into a house slowly and meticulously. To some degree, my life was represented by that house. I, too, was one dimensional and shabby inside and out. I needed work, remodeling, expanding, and a fresh coat of paint, so to speak. In retrospect, I needed to change my thinking because our lives are always a reflection of our thinking. I needed to rise above my circumstances.

I was a Marine, a bouncer, wanted by the police, violent, and dishonest when it fit what I wanted. I came complete with a gigantic chip on my shoulder. Then I found her. You know what I mean. Her! When Vickey walked into my life, I was introduced to the only person who would help me turn my life around and keep me from death or prison. She helped me overcome my past, make my present much better, and create a brighter future. Her love was the only love I didn't abuse or take for granted. It is genuine, believing, supporting, trusting, and without agenda. She brought out things in me I never knew were there. She taught me that the answer to "How?" is "Yes!"

You see, I was a "willing" victim. I just lived what others projected for me. I didn't think on my own and take charge of my life. I was a coward who was afraid to do anything but work so I could afford to party. Secretly, what I really wanted was to be happy and secure like others I observed. But I didn't know how to go about it. It makes me nauseous to even write that down on paper. That has to be one of the biggest excuses known to man. What do we mean when we say, "We don't know how"?

All my life, I had accepted on the outside what others said about me. On the inside, I dreamed of a better life, but I thought I was too unworthy to have one, let alone make it come true. Here I was, twenty-three years old, having survived amazing odds, still letting others dictate my life! I had been saying no to the best choices and opportunities, and I never rose above where I was. I was barely treading water. Maybe it's not so much the "How?" we fear. For me, it was the grit, hard work, and determination needed to finally say "Yes!" and embrace a better life.

I married Vickey, went to college, and graduated in 1976. In fact, beyond that, I continued taking college courses, the last being in 1995. How is it that I could go through so much and go on to live my dream? I said, "Yes!" Because of that, and my persisting, I am privileged to live the life I saw and wanted as a teenager. I will spend the rest of my life preaching the gospel and encouraging others to resist the negativity of non-accomplishers—and go on and make their dreams come true too.

How does someone overcome an abusive past? How can the weight of feeling unworthy be lifted? What can get us to see that we are not meant to be our own worst enemy, but, rather, our own best friend?

Begin curing those maladies by applying: The answer to "How?" is "Yes!"

Until we step out and move beyond the shadow of self-doubt, we will never take a step up and over. Say "Yes!" to the great things life has in store. Don't be hindered by the excuse of asking "How?" and getting stuck there. Those who ask "How?" without answering "Yes!" will never break free of limits. They'll never realize what could have been. How sad....

"You are more than smart enough to get into the game of life and head toward the end zone of your dream. Give life your best, rather than just letting the time run out on life's clock. You are more than smart enough not to die with your dream still locked inside of you!"

—Jack Smith

Chapter Five

You're More than Smart Enough to Make It Happen

"You can't possibly win unless you're in the game."
—Jack Smith—

"Men," said the coach, "we've worked hard to get to this game. I'm very pleased with how well you've played, and I know we can win with Johnny's strong arm. He's been an All-State quarterback for us the past two years, and we need to block for him so we can win the state championship tonight."

This was the most exciting night in the lives of these high school athletes. Play hard and fair, and they could be champions for the first time in the school's history. No doubt Johnny was the star of the team. Every major college wanted him on their campus. If he went down with an injury, all the coaches agreed that the task at hand would be hopeless.

Who's on the Sidelines?

The backup quarterback was Dave, who everyone made fun of and cruelly called "Dumboy". He'd never played a down in his entire football experience, but he was chosen because both the second and third stringers were out with injuries. He'd only been allowed on the team because his father was the school custodian and team bus driver. Admittedly, he wasn't the brightest student in school, but he had a better, stronger, and more accurate arm than even Johnny did. The coaches just didn't think Dumboy had what it took to lead the team.

The game started off badly as the opposing team ran the opening kickoff back for a touchdown. The first half ended with a score of 7-0. By the end of the third quarter, though, things looked promising—ending with Johnny's team still trailing at just 17-14. Then something happened that caused deep sighs, gasps, and moans from the sidelines to the stands. With but eight seconds remaining on the clock and one time-out, Johnny laid motionless on the field. He had been knocked out by a vicious but legal hit from a linebacker.

Getting into the Game

The coach had no choice. "Dumboy, come here!" he hollered. "Uh, yes sir," Dumboy said. Throwing his clipboard to the ground, the coach ordered, "Get in there and run the clock out." "Uh, what play do you want me to call?" Dumboy asked. Yelling back, the coach belted out, "Just call whatever you want! It won't make any difference—we can't win anyway." Dumboy nodded, put on his helmet, and ran awkwardly to the huddle.

"Hut one, hut two, hike." Taking the snap from the center, Dumboy was sacked almost immediately. He called time-out with three seconds left, infuriating the coach. The ball was resting on the 50-yard line with time for one play. Dumboy breaks the huddle and walks to the line of scrimmage for the last play of the game, and only the second play of his life. Trailing by three points with three seconds left is a tough situation even for the most experienced of players, let alone someone like Dumboy.

"Hut one, hut two, hut three, hike." Dumboy dropped back as if he'd played all his life. He threw a perfect spiral that hit the receiver with perfect timing as he crossed the goal line for the game-winning touchdown. The crowd went wild, and Dumboy was carried victoriously off the field and into the locker room.

"If I Was as 'Smart' as You…."

After hugging his family, the coach rushed to his team who was still celebrating with Dumboy as the center of attention. The coach asked, "Tell me, son, how did you know which play to call in that situation?" "Uh, I didn't," Dumboy replied. "I just looked across the line and saw number 67, so I added those two numbers together and called play number 15." "Are you kidding?" asked the coach. "Six and seven don't add up to 15." Dumboy just smiled and said, "Just think, Coach, if I was as 'smart' as you, we would have lost the game!"

That story speaks volumes about others setting limits which many seldom question and usually accept as true. But you're more than smart enough to get into the game of life and head toward the end zone of your dream. You won't listen to the would-be coaches who don't believe in what you bring to the game. You won't let those standing on the sidelines dictate your next play. You're going to break the huddle and give life your best, rather than letting the time run out on life's clock. You're more than smart enough not to die with your dream still locked inside of you!

Not So Dumb After All…

Do you realize that many of the world's brightest minds were once considered stupid or slow? Thomas Edison was kicked out of three schools by age nine and was considered unteachable. Sir Isaac Newton barely made it through grade school. Winston Churchill failed the eighth grade. Rocket scientist Werner Von Braun flunked ninth grade algebra. Albert Einstein barely survived high school math. Louis Pasteur struggled to pass chemistry, and Abraham Lincoln only made it through one year of formal education. There's hope for all of us! All of those people broke through the limits of others who labeled them as stupid.

Be Proactive!

I learned a long time ago that no one will look out for my interests or future like I will. When you understand that, then you're smart enough to do things that will make a positive difference in the lives of others as well as in your own.

Every business or profession has certain specific requirements for success. But all of them have one thing in common—the need to be proactive. As simple as that sounds, its meaning is profound. There'll always be those who venture into any business or profession with the philosophy that it'll be easy. Virtually everyone wants to be rich, and that's great. But there are those who want to be rich only if they don't have to do anything, letting everyone else do it for them. They don't take responsibility for their own success. They aren't givers nor are they proactive. Even if they've been given the knowledge, opportunity, and support necessary to create a better way of life, they fail to move forward. They're lazy. For example, there isn't a single successful business or profession you could find where someone just stated they were starting it, did nothing, and instantly became rich!

Like a football player, either break the huddle, jump on the pile, punt, pass, run, kick, or block, but *do* something! Otherwise, you're just kidding yourself that you'll succeed. You can't possibly win unless you're in the game! And yes, you're plenty smart enough to lead yourself and others to victory.

"*Like a football player, either break the huddle, jump on the pile, punt, pass, run, kick, or block, but do something! Otherwise, you're just kidding yourself that you'll succeed. You can't possibly win unless you're in the game! And yes, you're plenty smart enough to lead yourself and others to victory.*"

—Jack Smith

"**T**o be free is not merely to cast off one's chains, but to live in a way that respects and enhances the free-dom of others."

—Hyrum Smith

—*Chapter Six*—

Your Past Isn't Your Potential

*"Know that you, too, can grow, become,
and obtain as others have."*
—Jack Smith—

W e've lived much of our lives knowing we need to prepare for tomorrow. However, many wait until the last 10-20 years before they expect to retire to start setting aside funds for a comfortable living. Others don't prepare at all. How many times have you said or heard, "Man, why didn't I begin this earlier"?

There are basically three ways to prepare for your financial future: One is to let someone else, like an employer, or the government do it for you. Two is for you to prepare for it yourself. Three is a combination of both. What play are *you* following?

Recognizing Potential

Your past isn't your potential. Don't be limited by thinking your previous mistakes will be the rule for all of your tomorrows. The past is like water spilt on dry ground; it can't be picked up and put back into the glass. As you move forward, you'll create more successes to build on. This'll help boost your belief level. You need to *believe* you can, at least a little bit, to start off with, before you can honestly say "I'm doing it." Remember, you were created to become the best you can be.

Many wonder what their potential is or even if they've got any at all. The story is told of a finely dressed elderly statesman who was walking with the mayor, enjoying the sights, sounds, and smells of the city. As they came to a corner, a young boy ran past them—knocking the statesman off his feet—his elegant top hat tumbling to the ground. The mayor moved quickly, grabbed the young lad, and began to give him a well-deserved tongue-lashing.

Taking a deep breath to clear his head and putting his top hat back on, the statesman slowly rose to his feet and asked the mayor to let the boy go. "What?" asked the mayor. "Do you mean to just let this wild young boy get off scot-free?" The elderly statesman then did something quite unexpected: Standing erect, tipping his slightly dented hat, and bowing at the waist, the older man said, "Please excuse me, young man." To this the boy just stuck out his tongue and ran off.'

"Sir, why did you tip your hat to someone who could well have given you the proper respect?" the puzzled mayor inquired. Watching until the boy ran out of sight, the statesman turned and explained, "I tipped my hat on behalf of the young man's potential." "But he's just a street urchin and a wild one at that," the mayor insisted. Smiling, the statesman continued, "Sir, what we, as adults, seem to forget, is that all great men and women were, at one time, just six-year-old children with potential."

Measuring Potential

So how does anyone measure potential? Some people use tests to determine it but there's a lot more to it than that. Tests results can be false indicators because they don't measure desire and determination.

Naysayers abound and they love to put people down who are in the process of becoming top achievers. But those who persistently follow their dream until they realize it prove them wrong. For example, Clint Eastwood was told he would never make it in acting because his Adam's apple was too big. Charles Bronson was told he couldn't make it either. Elvis was sold from the Sun label for a mere $35,000 only to become one of the greatest recording stars in history. In all of these examples, what each person was told in the past didn't deter them from succeeding in the future. Desire and determination always win the day—as long as you don't quit.

One Sunday when I first started preaching, I was greeting the people as they came out of the church. A fellow stopped, shook my hand, and commented, "Young man, don't worry that you can't preach; you're still young." I was devastated, but later realized that that fellow, in his own awkward way, was telling me to never give up and that better days were ahead. Everyone who rises to the top was once at the bottom.

Broken by the Past

Most of us have either been to a circus or have seen one on TV. It used to bother me every time I'd watch the elephants. I couldn't figure out why they didn't just run away. They were so big and powerful, and yet each one of them was bound by only a small rope tied to a stake in the ground. The elephants could have, at any time, just pulled up their stakes and been on their way.

Tethering elephants and their accepting this as a limit to their freedom is similar to the limits we may put on ourselves in one or more areas of life. Long before an elephant is ever attached to the rope at the circus, the animal is bound by heavy leg chains from which he or she constantly tugs in an effort to get free. This process goes on as long as it takes for the elephant to stop trying to break the limit of the chains—in effect, to be "broken." When this happens, their past becomes their potential.

Many people are stymied in their quest for success because they, too, have been broken. They allow the fear of future failure that came from the failure of past exertions to numb their minds, therefore, never developing their full potential. Why? They never persevered long enough to break through the mental shackles of the past. All they have is a history of unsuccessful, often-feeble attempts

to break through and accomplish something. As a result, they don't believe they can attain what others whom they admire have attained. They believe their past is their potential, and that becomes their reality. They don't realize that so-called failures are simply learning experiences. Anyone who succeeds goes through many of them and grows in the process.

They Wouldn't Let Others Get Them Down

A young scientist who refused to admit failure said, "We haven't failed yet; we now know 1,000 things that won't work, so we're that much closer to finding what will." His name was Thomas Edison and aren't we glad he didn't believe his past was his potential in developing the light bulb?

Being avoided by his classmates and called a misfit by the teachers would be enough to discourage many, but not this young man. He was so slow to learn that his parents thought something was wrong with him. In Zurich, Switzerland, he failed his first college entrance exam. He finally got into college and went on to be a scientist of significant renown. His name was Albert Einstein.

He was called "Carrot Top" and twice failed entrance exams into a military academy. With much help, he made it in on his third attempt. The past wasn't going to be Winston Churchill's potential; a nation was saved and the world was inspired by his brilliance.

A man was expelled from Oxford and driven away from home by his father because he proclaimed support for freedom of speech and worship. Five times this man went to prison because of his beliefs. He came to America and lived in Philadelphia. Now the entire state is named after him. His name was William Penn. He refused to let his past interfere with his future—like Edison, Einstein, and Churchill.

Don't Drown in Your Potential

As the story goes, a young man once approached a great philosopher and asked how he gained such wisdom. Much to the boy's surprise, the philosopher suddenly grabbed him, pulled him over to a nearby fountain, and shoved his head under the water. Holding the earnest inquirer under the water for some time, the wise man just smiled and winked at a surprised passerby. Finally the philosopher let the fellow up—spitting, sputtering, and gasping for his next breath. "Why did you do that?" the seeker blurted out. "I almost drowned!" Laughing loudly, the philosopher replied, "Young man, when your thirst for knowledge is as great as your thirst for air was just a moment ago, you'll be on your way." Many fail by allowing themselves to be held under their potential, as they have done in the past. Don't let yourself or anyone else drown your potential, and don't drown the potential of those who may look to you for leadership and guidance either! You never know who's watching you!

"Every-one who rises to the top was once at the bottom."

—Jack Smith

"**W**hen seeking a lifelong dream, submission to it always comes before any victories—before the achievement day. Take charge of who you are, and, every day, do your best to get closer to the person you were meant to be."

—Jack Smith

—*Chapter Seven*—

Are You Working Toward Your Achievement Day?

"Genuine achievement involves more than money—
it goes deeper than the bottom line. It's about adopting
a better way of being, living, and serving."
—Jack Smith—

As usual, the employees had gathered at the local restaurant for lunch. At this point, the day's work routine was interrupted for a welcomed break in the action. Bob, a likeable man in his early 40s, had been with the company for a little more than two years. He was always on time and stayed as long as necessary, without extra pay, to get the job done. His superiors couldn't help but notice. This was a special day and everyone knew it but Bob.

The company owner had passed the word that, at lunch, he would honor Bob with an achievement award for his dedicated service to the company, and give him a position of greater responsibility.

Opportunity Missed

The company owner was in line a few places behind Bob so he could pick up the tab. Everyone was enjoying the conversation, meal, and anticipation of their co-worker's well-deserved award. But nothing happened! After lunch, the company owner stood up and thanked everyone for helping his business do better than ever. But not even one word was directed toward Bob. Everyone was looking at one another, puzzled.

What occurred that afternoon really caused the water-fountain gossip to kick into high gear. Why was Bob fired? No one found out until later that day. Bob's boss had seen Bob hide a three-cent pat of butter under his plate and later commented, "How could I trust someone with my business and millions of dollars if he can't even be trusted with a three-cent pat of butter?"

Many have had the opportunity for several achievement days in their lives only to compromise their integrity on something as silly as a three-cent pat of butter. Some compromise their success by accepting mediocrity and being stuck in the grind, as some call it. Still others compromise their futures by giving in to the fear of rejection. Achievement day and a better life would have been just around the corner, but they allowed fear to keep them at the bottom of Mt. Achievement. Have you ever donned the attire to scale Mt. Achievement, taken the opportunity and tools, and made it to base camp—only to quit and go back down to the bottom?

Who Wants A Better Life?

If you missed an achievement day, be encouraged and make a fresh new start. Keep working toward it. Embrace the opportunity for real accomplishment. Pull out all the stops to make it a reality.

Real achievement involves more than money—it goes deeper than the bottom line. It's about adopting a better way of being, living, and serving. It's taking charge of who you are and, every day, doing your best to get closer to the person you were meant to be. It's taking charge of your future and making the effort required to create the life you've always dreamed of. Gain the freedom to enjoy the independence you've always wanted. Claim what you could have accomplished earlier had you broken through your old self- or other-imposed limits.

So Close—*Yet So Far Away*

What's sad is that some who have the chance to reach financial freedom, or at least a better quality of life, just let it slip away. They think it will always be there and that *someday* they'll do it. They fail to seize the power of the moment. For example, thirty miles from Auburn, California is Sutter's Mill where the 1849 gold rush began. Thirty miles on the other side of Auburn is another site, though not quite as popular. In a cave there they found the body of John Marshall—the man who discovered Sutter's Mill. He, unfortunately, had never filed a claim for his find, and left this world sick, broke, and without the treasure that was well within his grasp. Couldn't some of those folks have pitched in and given him a little hope from the gold nuggets they gathered? Of course, but they didn't! It had been up to John to...

...File the Claim

Are you making the mistake of neglecting the opportunity that is right in front of you? John Marshall paid a dear price for it, and no one seemed to notice or care that he let his achievement day pass him by. It was his responsibility to take ownership of what could have been his, had he not let it slip away. Don't be like John and never file your claim. Don't wait idly by and watch others step in and reap the rewards that you could lay claim to.

File the claim in the office of your own heart so you can mine for the gold. First comes the surveying or prospecting, then filing the claim, and last of all the digging—making the required effort. Honestly survey your situation, then file the claim to be better tomorrow than you are today. How deeply are you willing to dig in order to ensure your own achievement day?

When seeking a lifelong dream, submission to it always comes before any victories—before the achievement day. Take charge of who you are, and everyday, do your best to get closer to the person you were meant to be.

Even Though They Said He Was Crazy...

Marvin Phillips, in his book *You Can't Fly to Heaven in a Straight Line,* tells the story of Garson Rice of Greensboro, North Carolina. He made headlines for selling a world's record 904 Toyotas in a single month. This was an amazing feat, especially considering it took him a whole year to sell 120 cars twelve years earlier! As a result, he had lost his financial backing and people told him he was crazy for selling anything from Japan. Garson wasn't a quitter; he pushed forward with his dream. He not only wanted to succeed, he thoroughly intended to do so.

Garson started the three-year, 100,000 mile guarantee. He believed in advertising and said that doing business without it was like winking at your wife in the dark. You knew what you were doing but she didn't. His seven keys to success are:

1. Persistence
2. Expectation
3. Concentration
4. Enthusiasm
5. Excellence
6. Advertising
7. Caring About People

Not only can you not fly to heaven in a straight line, you can't find your way to financial success that way either. There will always be obstacles threatening to impede your progress. As Phillips says, "They don't write articles about 'Negative Nellies.'" They write about world record holders like Garson Rice. Start flying and you'll reach your achievement day too.

"**W**ork toward your achievement day. Embrace the opportunity for real accomplishment, and pull out all the stops to make it a reality."

—Jack Smith

"**M**any people know what they want but make no preparation. They never grow or change their habits so they can go in the right direction. How about you? Is the direction you're heading going to take you where you want to be?"

—Jack Smith

Chapter Eight

Scarecrows Don't Get Anywhere!

"If you don't do it, who's going to be successful for you?"
—Jack Smith—

Never try to make up for a lack of faith in yourself by curling up in a warm electric blanket. That's where you set the controls for your ideal comfort level, while pushing aside the opportunity for a better life. You haven't yet achieved the life you desire, but you're comfortable.

I have two wonderful daughters. When those tiny little arms first clung to my neck, I knew I had to shift out of neutral with my life. Would I be Mr. Scarecrow or Mr. Take Charge?

Get Out of the Garden

Some children tell their parents they want to be just like them when they grow up. However, whether we have children looking to us for guidance or not, we can't afford to be the family scarecrow. Mr. Scarecrow is in the garden stuck where he is—not doing anything wrong but not being very productive either. Whatever he accomplishes with all his tomorrows has to come *his* way because he'll never venture out of his owner's garden nor does he have the ability to do so. He looks alive but there's a vast difference between just looking alive and really living—so step out and work hard to be what and where you want to be in the future. The person who aims at nothing hits the bullseye every time. Hitting nothing doesn't require doing anything.

On Career Day in high school, a friend and I were asked what we wanted to do after graduation. I'll never forget his answer: "I want to be a bum." Everyone laughed, thinking it was a joke. "No," my friend continued, "really, that's what I've always wanted to be."

The last I heard from him, he was successful for a bum, which was pretty much what he had become. He's a scarecrow. He wants to be noticed while putting out as little effort as possible to keep his job, survive, and pay the bills.

Prepare for Your Dreams

Again, we'll never be more successful than we are now without a great work ethic. As a kid, Mickey Mantle used to practice batting by hitting an old tire suspended on a rope—500 times a day. After his career was over, someone asked Mickey if he would have done anything differently in preparing for it. He responded, "I would've hit that tire 1,000 times instead of 500!" Mickey knew what he wanted, focused intently on it, and took action to prepare for the successful realization of his desire.

Many people know what they want but make no preparation. They never grow and change their habits so they can go in the right direction. How about you? Is the direction you're heading in leading to where you want to go?

Why do nations with lotteries raise such enormous amounts of money? Most people dream of being wealthy. It's easier to buy a ticket, even with odds of millions-to-one against ever winning, than it is to exert effort where the outcome depends on us. When we boldly take action in the direction of our dreams, the rewards will be much better than just winning the lottery. What we become as people, in and of itself, makes us rich.

Ten Questions on Success

Take a moment now, pull out a piece of paper, and write down the answers to these questions:

1. What's your main dream, goal, or objective?
2. What will it take to get there?
3. Are you willing to pay the price?
4. What will you do once you've achieved it?
5. Do you believe in YOU and your ability to make it happen?
6. If you're a scarecrow, how does it feel to be stuck in someone else's garden?
7. Is the direction you're heading in going to take you where you want to be according to what you want to accomplish in life?
8. What might be keeping you from heading toward your goal? Could it be an area where you need to grow?
9. Years from now, will you be sorry if you really didn't give your best effort to an opportunity you may already have?
10. If *you* don't do it, then who's going to be successful for you?

"No!" Always Leads to "Yes!"—*as Long As You Keep Going*

Scarecrows belong in the garden at the intersection of "Do Nothing" and "Just for Show." How about coming alive and growing your own garden?

Some may say they're afraid to hear "No!" But just think about it for a second. We've all heard "No!" thousands of times since we were babies until we left home, and beyond. And even though we've heard it over and over again, we grew and matured anyway, didn't we? Hearing "No!" didn't stop us from growing up and becoming adults.

The same is true when it comes to hearing "No!" in the business arena. You'll never meet a successful person who hasn't been told "No!" many, many times. That's just the way of success. Disappointing as it is, everyone is not ready to say "Yes!" at least not at the moment. Hear enough noes though, and you'll eventually start hearing yeses.

Do whatever it takes to get out of just standing still like a scarecrow in someone else's garden. Come alive! Start tilling, planting, and harvesting your *own* garden. The journey from scarecrow to success begins when you take charge and say "Yes!" If you're tempted to say it's too late, remember the words of Mahatma Ghandi: "It's not too late at all. You just don't yet know what you're capable of."

"It's not too late at all. You just don't yet know what you're capable of."

—Mahatma Ghandi

"The best way to become financially free is to help others. When we have the knowledge we need to become wealthy, we're responsible for giving it to others. Holding on to the knowledge is selfish and won't do us or anyone else any good!"

—Jack Smith

—Chapter Nine—

Is Giving a Secret to Success?

"What is it that you have to give
that can enrich the lives of others?"
—Jack Smith—

He rode into the small farming community in a long, luxurious black limousine. Everywhere he went in this small town, heads turned. He had grown up here but hadn't been back since he was 18. That day, though, he was the featured speaker at the church where he had regularly attended. It was their annual homecoming, and his topic was about being more successful. He was the best speaker they could have brought in. After all, he was a kind-hearted, philanthropic multimillionaire, and had been highly-esteemed and the talk of the community for many years.

His limo pulled up to the church right on time, and out of it he confidently rose with not a wrinkle in his finely tailored suit. His hair was impeccably styled and perfectly in place. His smile glistened brightly in the sun, revealing remarkably straight, white teeth. He was soon surrounded by members and visitors, alike, of this small quaint church that had an average attendance of sixty. But today, over two-hundred people had excitedly flocked to hear him, and extra chairs had been placed in the aisles.

Should You Be a Greater Giver?

After the minister's introduction, the man graciously began: "Ladies and gentlemen, it's a privilege to stand before you as we celebrate another homecoming. As you may know, I've been away more years than I care to count. I've been asked to speak about how to become successful, and I'm humbled and thrilled to have this opportunity. I'll make it real simple."

Pointing to a pew up-front, he continued, "That's where my folks and I used to sit every Sunday. What changed my life, and I remember it like it was yesterday, was when we had a visiting missionary in to speak one Sunday evening. He talked about all the missionary work that was being done in the country where he was sent, and how poor the people were. He also shared about how, with additional funding, so much more good work could be done.

"There I sat, a 15-year-old boy who had worked hard in the cotton fields with my parents. After buying clothes and shoes, I had one silver dollar left. I carried it, with a wonderful sense of accomplishment, in the top pocket of my overalls. I really wanted to keep that dollar but, on this particular day, as the collection plate was passed, I felt compelled to give it to the missionary. No one forced me to do it. My conscience wouldn't let me hold onto it. After all, I had been so blessed with the new clothes and shoes I was able to buy the day before.

"I felt like a million dollars when my beaming parents hugged me and told me how happy they were with me because of my generosity. I learned a valuable lesson that day. It's definitely better to give than receive. Friends, one of the secrets to success is to be a giver. I gave all the money I had on that day, and am doing my best every day to be a generous giver. I follow the promptings of my conscience and always act on my intention to do the right thing in all areas of my life. I stand before you tremendously blessed. I can hardly believe that I'm the richest man in the state and one of the richest men in the country. Be a greater giver, big of heart, as you care about and help others. You will be blessed."

What Is the Right Thing to Do?

All the people cheered and applauded—that is, all but one. An elderly gentlemen seated in the front row raised his hand. After several moments, the preacher noticed him and encouraged him to stand up and speak. "Sir, do I understand you correctly?" the older gentleman began. "Are you telling us you became a multimillionaire because you gave that one dollar to the missionary?" the older man asked. "Yes," replied the guest speaker. "Then sir, with all your millions, I dare you to give it all away again!"

There was complete silence for a few seconds, and then the audience began laughing. The elderly man was the only one who had the courage to challenge what the speaker was saying—which, if taken at face value, seemed to make little sense. Both giving and blessings are not meant to be just singular actions. They're to be ongoing cycles.

Smiling, the speaker calmly responded, "It all started there. The seed of greater generosity was planted in my heart like I'm now planting it in all of yours. The immense joy and gratitude I felt after giving that one dollar convinced me to be a lifelong giver—of myself, my compassion for the entire human family, and my talents and skills." He further explained that the giving can best be done by taking full advantage of the opportunities we all have every day to serve and make a difference. These are to be continuous events throughout each day. For example, if you're building a business or career, it would include meeting new people, taking an interest in them, finding out what their needs and desires are, and sharing how you could possibly assist them.

"Bloom where you're planted," as they say. Always look for ways you can help. We give back because it is the right thing to do and our pleasure to do so—not just so we can get more. True, blessings do follow but not if our hearts aren't right. Our lives aren't blessed just because we give when we're fifteen and never give again. We're blessed at any and all ages by giving.

Fakes Are Easily Spotted—*Be of Substance, Not Image*

Those in any upstanding, moral business or profession need to honestly believe that what they have to give to others is the best product, service, or opportunity around. Fakes are spotted and weeded out rather quickly in the business arena. Someone may be like a billboard that looks great when approaching but, upon further investigation, has little substance beyond the façade. It might be discovered that he or she is a sham with nothing of value to give to help others—in big or small ways. That person would only be projecting an image of benefit, and most people are motivated by substance—proven success, not just the appearance of it. If it's an opportunity you're sharing and you're not yet very successful yourself, this example can come through your leader, mentor, or other successful people in your business or career, until you become more successful yourself.

People tend to want two things—truth and hope. When offered with integrity and caring, we're on the way to financial freedom or whatever our dream may be. We, as people who uphold high ethical standards, are a significant part of whatever we are offering others. We are a part of the gift and the giving. Reach out in friendship to help others achieve their goals and dreams, make their lives easier, or overcome a challenge. As long as we have something genuine to share, those who are interested will soon discover we are the real thing, not fakes.

Do You Use a Big Scoop or a Little Scoop?

We don't need to give it all away to be successful, but we do need to give. We are rewarded by what we give in time, talent, care, money, and in other ways. It is the "big-scoop/little-scoop" way of thinking. Since we are rewarded based on how much heartfelt giving we do, why would we even consider using a little scoop? In fact, give me a bulldozer. Are you in?

Whenever the word giving is used, some immediately think of just money. Sure, it can be money, but let's dig more deeply into the fuller meaning of giving. As a minister, indulge me for a moment as I refer to the Bible. In Acts 3, you'll find Peter and John encountering a man crippled from birth. The man was taken to the temple gate to beg for money. But Peter responds, instead, with healing: "Gold and silver have I none but what I have I give you. In the name of Jesus Christ of Nazareth, walk."

Now, I am in no way equating what we have to give with the immensity of what God has to give. The point is that our giving is not always monetary. It may be the sharing of knowledge, our product, service or opportunity, books, prayers, hugs, encouragement, or an assortment of different things. Remember, people who are hungry don't want information; they want food. People who are serious about becoming financially free don't want a copy of a millionaire's bank statement but knowledge about how he or she became successful so they can duplicate it.

Who Else Might Want or Need What You Have to Offer?

Giving is about filling a want or need of the receiver, which, in turn, enriches the giver. It is a key secret to success and happiness. First of all, is what you are giving filling a need of yours? Then how about generously sharing it and filling the needs of others? If what you have to share or give away has blessed, thus bettered your life, then it would be your pleasure to pass it on, wouldn't it? *Pay It Forward*, as the movie is titled. Give to those what you've been given. To clear up any confusion, here's an example: The best way to become financially free is to help others. When we have the knowledge we need to become wealthy, we're responsible for giving it to others. Holding on to the knowledge is selfish and won't do us or anyone else any good!

Will You Step Over the Line?

In 1836, one-hundred and eighty-four men lost their lives at the Alamo. It's said that, one day, Colonel Travis walked in front of his men and unsheathed his sword. He then drew a line on the floor of the Alamo and asked, "Who among you is willing to step over this line and die with me?" Every man went across that line—even Jim Bowie, who was wounded and on a cot, was carried over the line to take his place with the other men.

Most of us don't need to give up our lives in military service. However, giving every day in service to others is essential to achieve our dreams of more personal freedom. Giving is the key to freedom in anything. Free nations enjoy the freedoms they have only because so many have given the ultimate sacrifice.

What do you have to give that can enrich the lives of others? No one ever becomes financially independent unless they have been supported by others in their quest. For example, others may have given advice, money, knowledge, contacts, or just moral support. I challenge you, starting today, to be even more generous in spirit. Open-mindedly give whatever it is you have to share as often as you can—with no expectations attached—then watch the positive results come pouring into your life.

"**O**pen-mindedly give whatever it is you have to share as often as you can—with no expectations attached—then watch the positive results come pouring into your life."

—Jack Smith

"Make no little plans; they have no magic to stir the blood and probably themselves will not be realized. Make big plans; aim high in hope and work, remembering that a noble, logical [plan] once recorded will not die."

—Daniel H. Burnham

—Chapter Ten—

So What Is Success Anyway?

"Set goals that require you to stretch—aim high. No one cares
about your success as much as you do."
—Jack Smith—

How will you know when you're successful? Some people say it all depends on how you define it. Sure, success is the progressive realization of a personally worthy ideal, dream, or goal, but it's more than that. Truly successful people also have peace of mind, good health, caring relationships, personal fulfillment, strong faith, and financial freedom. They've transcended their so-called limits to attain an extraordinary life with those elements in place!

Think about it. Without good health and peace of mind, you can't enjoy the fruits of your labor. Without caring relationships, you have no one to share it with. Without personal fulfillment and strong faith, you'll have a sense of frustration and emptiness. Without financial freedom, you're always concerned about having enough money to meet your wants and needs, and you're beholden to financial institutions.

When successful people reach a goal, they always set a new one. Why? They have a need to keep the progressive realization going. They understand that success is a process, not a destination. Unsuccessful people probably aimed too low to begin with or didn't even aim at all—allowing their supposed limits to stop them. They may not have had much belief in themselves that they could achieve what they really wanted. They may not have had enough faith that they were put on this earth to excel and be successful.

One place where I was preaching, we had a men's retreat to revitalize our enthusiasm. About halfway through the weekend, we got pumped and started setting new goals. One of the deacons suggested, "Let's set a goal of having 1,000 in weekly attendance within the next five years."

Blowing the Soot Out!

I loved the deacon's enthusiasm but this congregation had been around since the 1930s and had never averaged more than 183 on Sunday mornings. They reduced the 1,000 figure to what they thought was a more feasible 300. The elders had faith that this increase could be realized, but they would need to rally the congregation to the cause.

One deacon suggested that before we made a push to get 300 we could have a special "Friends Day," inviting our families, friends, and neighbors. As another deacon put it, "Let's really get busy and blow the soot out of our lackadaisical faith." We had set the goal date, but hadn't yet decided on a number. I sat there in amazement at these previously unenthusiastic men who were now all excited. So, what number did they pick to blow the soot out? 200! Yes, that's what I said.

Now keep in mind, we were already averaging 183, and 20-plus men were going to be involved in this push to build the church membership. Together, with their wives and the other members we'd contact, we thought we'd have a fantastic Sunday crowd in just two or three weeks. Those men sat there and, even in all their fervor, they would consider it a successful Friends Day if only 17 above our regular attendance showed up. I looked at them in shock and said, "Men, isn't that just a tad bit low?" "Hey," they responded, "let's make sure we reach this goal so people get excited."

Aim Low and You'll Put Failure in Motion

We had only 199 that Sunday. That's right, 199 on that soot-blowing, going-all-out, never-seen-anything-like-it-before Sunday! What was the problem? The goal was set so low that setting it simply wasn't motivating. Why? It wasn't big enough to fire people up and get them moving. A token effort would've accomplished it. If 17 people each brought one person that Sunday, then 166 didn't have to do a thing. What we had, in effect, was most members just watching to see who would do the work.

A similar situation could exist if we don't do much, if anything, and just expect those working for us or associated with us to build our business or careers. It doesn't work that way, and it even sounds ridiculous, doesn't it? Sure, once we get momentum going, others can help us carry the ball, as they duplicate us. But if we aren't positively productive examples, what are they likely to duplicate?

Rather than set high goals, we had aimed low and, therefore, put failure in motion. We wouldn't have been successful, in a true sense, even if we had realized that aim. Truth be told, my wife and I had three new people with us, and two other couples each had two with them. Now, let's do the math: That's seven new people between six recruiters. This means the remaining 177 brought a whopping ten new people—give or take a few, as perhaps not all the 183 originals were even in attendance that day! So regardless, we had failed. One of the elders commented, "Man, we only missed it by one. We'll do better next time." Guess what? For the duration I was there, next time turned into never.

True Success Is Wrapped in Integrity

Listen carefully to your leader or mentor so you can effectively duplicate what he or she has done to get where they are. Set goals that require you to stretch—aim high. No one cares about your success as much as you do!

You'll be successful and know it when you've done the work and produced the sweat it takes to get where you want to be. You'll know you're successful when you've achieved what you wanted.

However, success isn't genuine if a person has compromised his or her values, settled for less, or lied, cheated, or stole his or her way to the top. If someone's success isn't wrapped in integrity, that person has taken unfair advantage of others and is not a real success. He or she is a fraud and will eventually be found out. Besides, that's no way to live—always looking over your shoulder hoping you won't be caught.

Have you ever heard of Charlemagne who was buried sitting on his throne? His finger was pointed to the Bible on his lap—forever stuck on Matthew 16:26: "What shall it profit a man if he gains the whole world and loses his soul?"

So what are some characteristics of successful people? Husbands and wives who are loving and supporting of each other. Parents who are positive-thinking, responsible, attentive, affirming, encouraging, loving, and firm-yet-fair moms and dads. They don't buy their kids more stuff or give them more money in an effort to fulfill their parental duties. Successful people have their priorities in order and don't compromise their values or responsibilities for anyone or anything else.

See the Smiles

Keep your spiritual, financial, emotional, relationship, and physical goals in perspective. However, a periodic emphasis on one or more areas may be necessary to reach a major objective, so priorities need to be set accordingly. Prioritize goals with your family's input, then work together as a team to accomplish them.

When a goal is reached, you won't see destruction, disaster, or unnecessary disappointment. It was challenging, but you thoughtfully worked through each situation with kindness, character, and confidence. Real success will be reflected in the smiles of those you've influenced and helped. They'll be more successful and happy because you dared to set integrity-based goals and took action until you accomplished them.

"*Real success will be reflected in the smiles of those you've influenced and helped. They'll be more successful and happy because you dared to set integrity-based goals and took action until you accomplished them.*"

—Jack Smith

"Limits are only products of the imagination. Expand your thinking to include the achievement of your dream. Pursue it without letting the limited thinking of others stop you. You're destined for greatness."

—Jack Smith

—Chapter Eleven—
Not Limited by What Others Think

"Follow your dream rather than following
the crowd. Dare to do mighty things!"
—Jack Smith—

He was five-feet-six-inches tall and weighed in at 132 pounds. A victim of polio, his right arm was small and underdeveloped. Obviously, his stature wasn't menacing, but, nonetheless, he was very much anyone's equal when it came to self-defense. Many people underestimated his ability in competition, only to pay for it later! He refused to be treated differently because of his perceived handicap. When we had to throw 100 punches alternating our arms, he threw 100 with his left arm. When we'd do a certain number of blocks, he'd always double them.

I first met him when I signed up to take his tae kwon do classes. I, too, wondered what such a small man with one functioning arm could really do in a self-defense situation. After watching his technique, I knew I'd found something special in him. When I saw him spar against someone in the advanced ranks, he proved his reputed level of excellence. Not one to brag, he let his fine work speak for him.

No One Could Hold Him Back

Black Belt, then the top martial arts magazine, did an article on him. Something he said really struck me: "All I have to do to motivate in a classroom is stand there. Who's going to tell me they can't do something when they look at my disability?" He didn't let others set his limits nor use his physical challenge as an excuse—a great example for us all. Other people's negative attitudes about our potential are irrelevant. After all, everyone is entitled to his or her opinion, and it's really none of our business. So, instead of letting negative opinions stop us, let's use them as fuel to feed our engine of success.

Remember, no one cares as much about your dream as you do, which puts the responsibility for achieving it square in your lap! What if my tae kwon do teacher had let others dictate to him what he could and couldn't do? What if he had just felt sorry for himself?

As I mentioned, my teacher's admirable work spoke for him very strongly. I discovered this the hard way. When I made my First Degree Black Belt, he asked me if I knew about the initiation process. I told him I didn't. He said, "Well, now is as good a time as any." "Yes, sir," I replied, "what do you want me to do?" He motioned for me to come to the middle of the workout room (called the Dojo) and we bowed to each other. We sparred for a few minutes and it went fairly well. He asked me if I was enjoying myself and I said I was. I wasn't about to tell a Fourth Degree Black Belt that I didn't like what we were doing! He then asked, with a big smile, if I was ready for my initiation. Even though I was scared, I said, "Yes." I knew winners embraced challenge and I wanted to win.

I'd never been hit so many times in so many ways and so quickly. With utmost care and control, though, he didn't hurt me. When it was over he said, "Thank you for sparring with me. Never underestimate someone's potential or let anyone lead you to believe that you can't accomplish what you want in life. If I had been molded by what other's thought, I wouldn't have my own successful school. Instead, I'd be working for someone else and helping them make the money I wanted to have in my bank account."

We Are What We Live—*What Others Say Is Just Talk*

I have mostly always cared about what others thought, about me and what I was doing, even though I wouldn't admit it. But the fact of the matter is, the people you think are thinking about you, probably aren't! After all, they have their own problems and concerns to deal with. At first, this may be disappointing, but, in the long run, when you really think about it, it's liberating. So the good news is, go do what you need to do. No matter what, though, always be courteous, kind, and considerate of others. However, if people are disrespecting us, trying to stymie our dreams, and put down our potential, that's unacceptable. That's when we may need to part company.

I've been asked on several occasions whether my dream was always to be a preacher. I chuckle to myself every time and reply, "Growing up, the only religion I knew was being a heathen. Being a preacher was never my goal. Going to heaven was and is my real goal now, as it has been for the past 30-plus years. My preaching vocation developed en route to my goal."

Many share the same or similar goals. No matter what our ultimate goal is, life is a journey with twists, turns, and bumps. Our journey toward the end goal contains several other intermediate goals along the way. In fact, seldom, if ever, can one goal be reached without accomplishing others. Stick-to-it-iveness is, therefore, essential. The people who give up are plentiful and that's why they're called the masses. People who quit on themselves are everywhere and, sad to say, many lead lives of not-so-quiet desperation.

I've always had people trying to set limits for me. Perhaps they thought since something seemed impossible for them, then it was impossible for me too. Maybe they were projecting their own lack of confidence on me. Those who say they don't doubt you for a moment—it is just the dream they think is unreachable—are really saying that since they don't believe they can do it, then neither can you. This has nothing to do with *your* potential at all—just their own self-doubt. If you choose to believe it when they are basically dumping their accumulated programming of negativity on you, then you're allowing the limits someone else imposes on him- or herself to be yours too. Not only that, but you wouldn't be any further ahead than they are because both of you would be in a state of do-nothingness!

Believe It or Not…

As you know by now, the chances of someone knocking on your door and handing you a fortune are virtually zero. We all know various people. There's no telling how many I've come in contact with over the years. Yet, I know of only a few who've inherited a fortune and no one that has won one. How about you? No sweepstakes announcers, like those from Publishers Clearinghouse, have ever been in my neighborhood. However, the door of opportunity is there for all of us to knock upon and go through. I know several people who are independently wealthy. How did they get that way? They refused to allow someone else to set their limits. They also figured out that we all need to take advantage of the fine opportunity that we may already have and give it our all.

Her name is Margaret Louise Brickey. She attends church where I preach and is an inspiration to anyone with aspirations to achieve. Later in life, she began to fulfill her dream of writing children's books. She had a burning desire to share her story idea about a young bunny named Pouche (pouch-eee). He was born with a pouch and one ear was longer than the other. He never knew what his purpose was in life until the Easter Bunny couldn't make his rounds one year. Pouche steps in to assist only to discover that he himself is the real Easter Bunny!

She took her story to a hometown publisher who made a prototype copy of the book that, to put it kindly, was less than appealing to the eye. Louise, as we call her, was not deterred one iota by what others thought. She could let this be the end of her dream or keep believing there was something better out there. The publisher wanted to change several things, so she decided to go elsewhere. It took over eight years for it to finally happen but when it did, it happened big.

Louise and her husband had a farm that was slowly going under. They needed help or they would lose it all. Then all her hard work and effort paid off. Her book was seen by someone who believed in her talent and they flew her to the east coast where she visited several shopping malls to read her book to the children. She was an instant success and sold her rights to the book about Pouche for close to a quarter million dollars. The farm was saved and she and I are working on other children's books together. Now in her 70s, she is proving that she is not a one-dream person.

For many, if someone doubts them, they crawl back into their shell—feeling silly for wanting something more than they have, as if they don't deserve it. Regardless of what you endeavor to do, sure as the sun rises every day, someone will doubt whether you can accomplish it. What if the worst-case scenario happens and, in the end, you fall short of your goal? You still went for your dream, which was an adventure in and of itself, and is far beyond what most do in an entire lifetime. As long as you're able, you still have another chance. Follow your dream rather than following the crowd. Dare to do mighty things!

"**H**ow long will some-one sit in the same trap, in the same place, in the same pain, doing the same complaining about the same situation?"

—Jack Smith

Chapter Twelve

Bear Trap Anyone?

*"Those who really care about us will always
encourage us to get out of any trap we may be in."*
—Jack Smith—

His name is Walter, but we affectionately call him "Cob." He's the type of person who always gets back at you if you've done something he doesn't like. And believe me, he's the last person you'd want after you! He got his nickname, which is short for "rougher than a corn cob," because of something that happened when he was a boy.

Young Cob helped raise goats in the town of Hog Jaw, Arkansas. One day, a man known to be a rough customer came to buy a goat from Cob. The price was 50 cents. But after loading the goat, the man handed Cob only 25 cents. Cob said, "The price is 50 cents!" The man retorted, "Twenty-five cents is all the goat's worth, and that's all I'm paying." But messing with a kid named Cob was something he'd live to regret.

The man drove an old pickup, with the front seat so worn out that there was a hole on the driver's side big enough to see the springs. To make do, he had put a tattered old quilt over the hole. After the man had the audacity to put the goat into the back of his truck and then bully Cob into getting it at half-price, he walked away and went into the hardware store. Furious, Cob marched out to his shed and got a bear trap. While the man was in the store, Cob silently and carefully lifted that quilt and sat the trap down in the springs so it couldn't be seen. Looking up and seeing no one coming, he carefully placed the quilt back over the hole and quietly walked a short distance away.

Cob stood within view of the truck, smiling to himself, waiting patiently for the inevitable. Out of the store the older man came with that ever-present scowl, which would soon be replaced with a shocked look and a howl. As Cob later reported, "His hollering could be heard in the surrounding counties." Now you know how Cob got his name. Bear trap anyone? Me neither!

No Shortcuts

It's sometimes easy to fall into others' traps. Like the mean man in the story, we can be our own worst enemy. Some people push, shove, and try to bully their way to the top. The desire is there but the ill-intended approach gets them in trouble. They think they have outsmarted the opposition or situation—only later to be bitten by reality.

There aren't any shortcuts to success—it's a building process—which, unfortunately, many never learn. Then, too, supply and demand will always be around and so will this formula for success: Product + Priorities + Positivity + Perseverance + Performance + Payday = Financial Success. Are you using this formula, or is something missing?

Avoiding the "Bear" Trap

How do we avoid an up-close encounter with a bear trap? Take a fresh look and examine what naysayers may be telling us. Just because someone says something, doesn't mean we have to believe it. The choice is ours. Ask yourself these four questions if anyone says anything negative about you:

1. Is it true?
2. Is it true to everyone?

3. If it's true, why didn't I see it?
4. If it's true, how can I either fix it or compensate for it?

For example, a friend at work might have learned that you're building a business in your off-the-job time. He or she might be telling you that getting financially free is farfetched—that you're just a dreamer and wasting your time.

Let's run through the four questions:

1. *Is it true?* No! You decide it's only farfetched for people who either don't have a dream or aren't doing whatever it takes to make it happen. You know people who started their businesses with a lot less going for them and a lot more challenges than you have. They retired early from their jobs and live a lifestyle most can only imagine. Yes, you're a dreamer but you're committed to making those dreams come true.

2. *Is it true to everyone?* Farfetched is certainly not true. You have friends in business who encourage you to aim for exactly the lifestyle you want. Rather than shut you down when you've shared a dream, they've built you up. They also recommend tapes or CDs, DVDs, books, and various functions you can attend to keep your attitude positive and to stay on track.

3. *If it's true, why didn't I see it?* Farfetched is not true but we'll talk about it because many people who are embarking on a new exciting path will hear this excuse. You are on the move and your so-called friend isn't. He or she may be criticizing what you're doing because of jealousy. You're probably surrounding yourself with people who are on the go and optimistic about their bright new futures. Your friend could join you rather than criticize you, but may be afraid to do so. Perhaps a naysayer is trying to set limits for him or her, or their own internal dialogue of self-doubt is holding them back!

4. *If it's true, how can I either fix it or compensate for it?* Again, although farfetched is not true, we'll address it. Simply prove him or her wrong by blazing the trail to financial freedom. Maybe this will help the doubter. If that doesn't work,

however, be encouraged. You'll have plenty of new friends where you're headed who'll understand and support you.

Question the validity of any negativity being thrown your way. Don't use it as an excuse not to do what you need to do to move ahead. Sure, there may be people who don't believe in you or what you're doing, but that doesn't make them right. Those who really care about you will encourage you to get out of any trap you may be in. The sooner you figure out who those people are and how important they are to you, the better off you'll be.

Same Old, Same Old—*or Released from the "Bear" Trap*

Some put people in one of two categories: the haves and the have nots. Have you noticed that there are those who will step out and those who won't—those who are willing to stay in the bear trap for life and those who aren't content until they release themselves from it? A bear trap is anything that can be used as an excuse to never get out of it, get up, and get going. Now, I can just imagine some of you saying: "Well, Jack, sitting in a bear trap is painful and a real good reason to yell and complain." I couldn't agree more. But how long will someone sit in the same trap, in the same place, in the same pain, doing the same complaining about the same situation?

Remember, as tempting as they may seem, get-rich-quick schemes aren't the answer. Success requires dedicated work and relationship building. The man in the story who cheated the kid out of 25 cents was taking the "easy" way to financial gain, and everyone in the county knew about it in a short period of time. It didn't take long for him to pay for it by sitting in the bear trap, did it? His lack of integrity likely cost him a new pair of pants and maybe a couple of weeks of painful sitting too!

I have a friend who has been in and out of every imaginable "ground floor opportunity" that came along. He would start off like a house afire, fizzle out after a couple of months, and then inevitably move on to something else. This was his pattern and, to this day, he's still looking for a so-called ground floor opportunity—a quick fix.

Some people think the grass is greener on the other side of the fence, but when you get closer, you start seeing the weeds. Whenever you see someone who has attained his or her goal, you'll never find that person stuck in a bear trap.

"**M**ost people will never reach financial freedom working from 9 to 5. But with a great plan, a burning desire, and the focus and discipline to invest time and energy beyond their job, they can make it happen."

—Jack Smith

—Chapter Thirteen—

The Garbageman

"Plan your work and work your plan."
—Unknown

People would always make fun of "Cotton" who lived a few miles out of town on Pigeon Creek Road. You couldn't miss his house; it was the most rundown. The windows were knocked out, it had no electricity, and animals roamed everywhere inside.

Cotton never married and, as far as we knew, had few relatives around. I saw him on several occasions since he lived across the road from my grandmother. For as long as anyone could remember, it was Cotton who picked up their garbage. Every morning, he'd get up early and take his converted pickup around the county making the necessary stops for that particular day. Some pitied this "poor" man and couldn't imagine anyone living the way he did.

Invest in Your Dream

The truth eventually came out that Cotton had invested wisely. He had bought several hundred acres of land, and the county leased part of it for the garbage dump. This, combined with other rumored investments, had Cotton touted as one of the wealthiest people in town. It's reported that, upon his death, his estate was worth well

over a million dollars. Not too bad for a garbageman. Just goes to show you that you can't tell the worth of a person by his or her appearance or what they do for a living.

Now I know what you're thinking. I, too, have asked why would someone with so much wealth choose to live the way Cotton did? Cotton was just Cotton. He was who he was, take him or leave him. His goal was to be the best garbageman in the county, and he succeeded. He could laugh all the way to the bank at all the critics who talked behind his back.

Don't Laugh at Another Person's Dream

Becoming the best garbage collector in the county may not be your life-long goal, but it was Cotton's—and he became quite successful in doing so. His story is tantamount to a sermon I preached one Sunday on goals and success. I was trying to be funny by telling the congregation what I always told my daughters: I never wanted to visit them at their workplace in the future and have them ask me if I wanted fries with my burger. Sharing this sounded like a good idea at the time.

However, after services, a man walked up and said, "You know, flipping burgers and selling fries isn't a bad way to make a living." I had forgotten all about him. He owned a few restaurants in several towns and was very affluent. His goal was to flip burgers and sell fries better than anyone else in the area, and he was a success because of it.

Something someone rejects can be the vehicle to another's fortune. People may laugh at you for engaging in a new business venture or lifestyle and totally reject your plan. But sooner or later, you may well be laughing at their skepticism—all the way to the bank. The expression goes something like, "He who laughs last laughs longest!"

Stop Telling Them

Someone once told me, "I get so frustrated. Every time I tell my family something I've done to build my business and improve my life, they laugh at it and put me and the business down. What would you suggest I do?" I said, "Stop telling the family!" It was like I had attached an electrical wire to his face and I had shocked him to awakening his innermost being. His eyes opened wide, his mouth dropped, and he took a deep breath. He finally got it! It's okay to tell only those you really want to tell—those you're fairly sure care enough about you not to put you or your business down. Why tell people who are critical, short-sighted, or nonsupportive? It doesn't make sense, and it's only asking for trouble.

Never let anyone else set your limits by accepting his or her negative attitude toward you about anything. They can try, but can't really set your limits without your permission. Besides, it's *your* time, energy, and resources that you're investing to make *your* goal a reality. After all, they don't pay your bills, do they? You have only one life to live and your future starts in the next instant. Why would you have to settle for what someone else thinks is right for your life? You don't! The sooner you realize that, the better off you'll be.

The Seven "Ps" for Success

Here are seven steps for being successful in any endeavor:

1. Plan your plan.
2. Prepare for your plan.
3. Promise to follow through with your plan. (If you're not committed to it, neither will anyone else be.)
4. Promote your plan to others with whom you can relate.
5. Produce your plan so others can see your results and duplicate them.
6. Perfect your plan as needed in conjunction with your leader or mentor.
7. Perpetuate your plan as you reach one goal after another— always dreaming bigger.

Financial Freedom

Cotton, the garbageman, followed a plan that made him a millionaire. It wasn't my plan and it's probably not yours either. What was this incredible plan of his? Well, it went something like this: "If you're not making money while you're sleeping, then you're not making real money." Sounds great, but what does it mean? Simply put, it means that most people will never reach financial freedom just by working from 9 to 5. With a great plan, a burning desire, and the focus and discipline to invest time and energy beyond their job, they *can* make it happen.

It's amazing how quickly we can change our attitude about someone, isn't it? Cotton would just go about his business, whistling and singing all the time, and we would make fun of this "poor" man. Upon his death, we finally figured out why he was so happy. This man, who chose to be the best garbageman in the county, had honestly succeeded. Admittedly, during that time, whenever I walked into the bank, no one called *me* by my first name. But they did so for Cotton. Cotton was the millionaire trash taker, but I was just a trash talker. He ventured out and worked hard. I ridiculed and did nothing. As I said before, he aimed at his target and I aimed at nothing. We both hit our targets.

"**W**hat opportunity might you have at hand to work with others so that you can make your *dream* a reality?"

—Jack Smith

—Chapter Fourteen—

Fling the Door of Opportunity Wide Open!

*"Will we stay where we are and just
survive or will we venture out to achieve our dreams?"*
—Jack Smith—

How many times have you seen something that's making someone else a fortune and thought, "I could have done that"? The inventor of Post It Notes became very wealthy. Remember the Pet Rock craze, the Hula Hoop, Slinky, and the Frisbee? Like me, you may never invent anything. That's okay. Fortunately, we don't have to be that innovative to be successful.

Believing, Reaching, and Stretching

Many people are negatively influenced by others into believing that reaching and stretching to go beyond where they are is an exercise in futility. Fortunately, it's easy to identify the naysayers. They talk behind the scenes about what they could or should have done or are supposedly going to do, but they never actually do anything or certainly not very much. They've accepted limits set by someone else and used them as excuses to never go beyond where they are. They complain a lot but rarely do anything constructive to remedy the situation.

Naysayrers voice their opinions the loudest, smirk the longest, and stay where they are forever—or until they get booted out! They talk with great bravado and can be quite convincing, but, truth be told, they're probably too afraid to step out and become the best *they* can be. They allow themselves to be discouraged by the negative news and often make no effort to change.

Get Out of Port!

Thomas Aquinas said, "If the primary aim of a captain was to preserve his ship, he would keep it in port forever." This woke me up. I could have chosen to stay where I was and just survive, or I could venture out to achieve my dreams. My goal was to write. Whatever wealth may come as a reward of putting my heart and soul into living my dream would be icing on the cake. However, I could've stayed "at port" and been just fine in terms of comfort and stability. This may be true for you too. But what bothered me most was thinking about reaching old age and wondering "What if?". "What if I had written?"; "What if I had something to say that just might make a difference in other people's lives?"; "What if, by writing, I could make a difference in my life and that of my family?" It was obviously time to get out of port. How about you? Isn't it high time to get out of port?

We're All Important

Someone asked me if I've ever had an original thought. I had to admit that I couldn't think of even a single one. That's when he assured me this wouldn't determine whether I was successful or not. You see, some people are thinkers; some are inventors; some are advertisers; some are organization/business builders or other leaders; while others work for or associate with these people. All of us are important. Even the weakest contributor in any team effort is integral to its success. Sure, some people have more initiative and are more inventive than others but no one is really "self-made." No one becomes successful without associating with other people.

The invention of Post It Notes made someone very wealthy. But it didn't happen without others on the team doing their parts. Some one had to think it, invent it, advertise it, manufacture it, and get it to the customers. The same is true with your dream. Be inventive as to how you can best use your time, energy, and resources to make it come true. What opportunity might you have at hand to work with others so you can make your dream a reality? Advertise your dream to yourself every day in pictures and words posted where you'll see them often. Get to work, doing what's required, and step-by-step, make it happen. If you already have a system of success in your industry, follow it in a dedicated way, share it with others, and help them do the same. Become a leader in your field.

Someone Will Notice!

He had always wanted to play college football. By the time he was 14, he was six-feet, one-inch tall, but weighed-in at only 133 pounds. If he turned sideways and stuck out his tongue, he looked like a zipper! Nonetheless, he told some of the guys on the team about his dream, and they shared it with the others.

One day, everyone started making fun of him, laughing at the skinny kid who had dared to share his dream with non-dreamers. But by the time he was a senior, he weighed 155 pounds and could throw a football 65 yards. The coach said he had never before seen such an arm on a high-school kid. One day, negative teammates who had laughed at him before, pinned him down in the locker room and cut his hair, saying it was too long. Regardless, this still-skinny kid led the team to a very respectable season. He maintained his dream but now kept it to himself.

After graduation and with no college offers, he joined the Marines. While playing football, he was noticed by a major who never missed a game. The major asked the young man if he had ever considered trying out for college ball. Still keeping his dream to himself, he softly responded, "It had crossed my mind a long time ago." The officer said he could get him a tryout at his alma mater, but, sadly, it never happened.

Promote Yourself

You may think this is a sad ending to a story where someone had potential but would never be able to put it to use. But wait. Upon leaving the Marines and going back home, he and his brother went to the local football field to watch a practice. The coach asked the boys if they would like to dress out and play on the second team offense against the first team defense. They jumped at the chance.

Here were the rules: The brothers would have possession of the ball first and, if they scored, they would keep the ball. But if they didn't score, they'd have to play defense against the first team offense.

Well, the used-to-be-skinny kid played quarterback while his brother played tailback. Those second stringers never had as much fun as they did that day, guiding the second string to an impressive 56-0 win over the first-string defense. The coach was so impressed with the quarterback, fresh out of the Marines, that he contacted the local college and got him a full scholarship to play football.

The boy wasn't the greatest thinker nor did he invent football. He had only promoted himself to the people who could see him in action. His demonstration of skill made his dream come true. If he would've let someone intercept his dream and given up, he'd have always wondered what might have been. That young quarterback was me!

The previous long-time host of the *Tonight Show*, Johnny Carson, was ready to open the door of opportunity. In 1949, he graduated from the University of Nebraska and took a job at a local radio station. He was later hired in 1951 by KNXT, a Los Angeles station. This was his big break as his program, *Carson's Cellar*, which aired from 1951-53, was a favorite of the very well-known and respected comic, Red Skelton. In 1954, Skelton hired Carson to join his show as a writer. When Skelton knocked himself unconscious an hour before a live telecast was to begin, it was Johnny who filled in. John William Carson had gone from being "The Great Carsoni" doing magic tricks at age 14 to a television icon. Mr. Carson flung the door of opportunity wide open and went right through it to claim his dream.

There's a door of opportunity in front of you right now. Fling it wide open and walk through.

"No excuse is acceptable when it comes to achieving a dream. No excuse will help you break through fear and achieve it either!"

—Jack Smith

Chapter Fifteen

Have You Ever Been Really Afraid?

"Never live in fear and always remember that
your dream is too big for you to miss."
—Jack Smith —

I t was 1977 and I was asked to come to Slidell, Louisiana, to try out for a vacant preaching job. After the privilege of preaching and teaching, as well as attending the potluck lunch, the elders said they wanted to meet with me after evening services.

It was about 11 o'clock by the time my wife and I left the church that night. On the way home, we decided to stop at a convenience store for some snacks. Vickey stayed in the car while I was to make a quick trip into the store. As I approached the building, I saw this huge muscular man sitting on the bench outside. He was arguing with the woman beside him who appeared to be his girlfriend. He stared at me as I smiled and walked on in to purchase the goodies.

Facing Fear and Doing It Anyway

On my way out of the store, I saw that the couple who were on the bench were now standing and arguing. I looked up at him amazed—he was the biggest man I had ever seen! Under his left arm, he was carrying a six-pack of his favorite beverage, and it wasn't soda. You could tell he was already slightly inebriated. As soon as I walked through the door, he furrowed his brow, raised his long, powerful arm, and pointed his finger in my direction. Then he said words I'll *never* forget: "Honey, I think I can whip this guy!"

I was still smiling, oblivious that he was talking about me. I looked around to see who this giant was glaring at in preparation for a fight. Startled, I realized I was the only one standing there. He then started to lunge toward me. Sure, I could have smacked him with the bag of food, but why ruin perfectly good snacks? The girl-friend then stepped right in front of him and said something that was music to my ears: "Honey, you don't have to prove anything to me." "Alright," he said, his face softening, stumbling back a step or two, "but you know I could have taken him." She nodded in agreement.

From the car, my wife had been watching the unexpected turn of events. I looked at her and smiled sheepishly as I quickly stepped to the safety of the car. She didn't say a word as I sat down, fastened my seatbelt, and started the car. Right before we left the store parking lot, I stopped the car, looked at my sweet wife, and said, "Honey, you know, don't you, that I could have taken him?" She smiled, doing her best not to laugh at me, and said, "Just drive!"

When Giant Bullies Appear

We all face giants at one time or another. And just like my situation, they seem to appear at the most inopportune times. Some may face the giant bully called "time"; others, the giant bully called "lack of confidence." Then there is that ever-popular giant bully called a "round tuit." This one can take up residence in the mind, calling out "You don't have time for this dream-fulfilling stuff now. You're too busy taking care of the family and paying the bills." But this is nothing but naysayer nonsense!

All of us have said we would do something when we got a "round tuit." I had a great teacher who, on the first day of class, handed out pieces of paper, each cut in a circle with "TUIT" written on both sides. She warned: "This is for all of you who have the pro-pensity to make excuses in my class. Keep this gift to remind you that *no* excuse is acceptable to me for not doing your assignments."

One of the students asked what in the world it was that the teacher had just handed out. "It's a 'round tuit,'" she said." The next time you tell someone you'll do something when you get around to it, remember, I already gave you a 'round tuit.' So get moving!"

Fear Is Only an Excuse

Many excuses are the result of fear. I keep coming back to the word fear because we need to put fear into perspective. It's one thing to be afraid of a giant at a convenience store, but something entirely different to be afraid of things manufactured in the mind. For example, have you ever talked with a jealous person who projects every possible negative scenario onto his or her dating or marriage relationship? This is like someone who predicts failure and constantly makes excuses for never focusing on and working toward a goal. As one young man, just about to turn 21 said, "My daddy told me that if I had received a dollar from every person who had talked themselves out of being successful, I could retire on my birthday!"

Address any fear you may have by sharing it with someone who cares about you and is supportive of your desires—preferably a leader or mentor. Once you've brought the fear into the light, it'll start dissipating as you focus on how to handle it and begin to take action. For example, say you're afraid of meeting new people, which keeps you from finding more prospective associates. You share your concern with a leader who can guide you to books, audios, or DVDs/videos done by others who have overcome the same fear. They give you hope that you can conquer the fear, too, and follow the examples you've been given.

Be Committed to Your Success

Many continue to fear doing something because they're not yet totally committed to making it happen. Therefore they don't have the stick-to-itiveness to break through the fear. It's that way in business and all areas of life. Being successful often calls for being assertive—not pushy or phony, but forward thinking and proactive.

Some people shrink back, refusing to take on the challenge. Again and again, they end up just watching others make the breakthroughs needed to get to the next level or accomplish another goal. It seems that those who are committed to the status quo are always in the audience of life instead of with the go-getters on stage. They need to courageously step forward and take charge of their situation. All it takes are baby steps to break the inertia and get started. Once in motion, momentum can be built.

I have a friend in business who has been repeatedly honored in his field as top producer of the year. I asked him what the difference was between him and other businesspeople. He said, "Jack, I'm not afraid to be told 'No!'" He has confidence in what he has to offer and enthusiastically goes for it while not being attached to the outcome with any particular person. He's so honest, well-liked, and readily available to help those he serves that he has repeat customers who will only deal with him. He focused on his dream to be the number one producer, and he is. Failure may be a word in the dictionary but it's not an option in his life.

Dr. Karl Menninger, world-renowned psychiatrist, said, "Attitudes are more important than facts." Many times, successes and failures are determined by our attitude. Randy Simmonsin, in his book *What to Do When You Don't Know What to Do*, tells an interesting story from Paul Harvey: "Several years ago there was a rash of airplane hijackings in the United States, particularly out of the Miami airport. One such plane was hijacked out of Miami on its way to New York. The hijacker ordered, 'Turn the plane around and head for Havana, Cuba.' The pilot could tell the man was serious and desperate, so he did what the hijacker said.

"But a strange thing happened. When the gunman tried to intimidate the passengers, they laughed. They were loose and carefree all the way to Havana. They laughed while the plane was on the ground and while tense negotiations were going on between the American and Cuban authorities. They turned the whole experience into a big party.

"Only one man, other than the hijacker and the pilot, wasn't laughing. He didn't get the joke. In fact, he was worried that the hijacker would react violently to the laughter of the passengers. His name? Allen Funt, who, for many years hosted the TV show *Candid Camera*, which highlighted pranks and practical jokes. When the other passengers saw Allen Funt was on the plane, they assumed the hijacking was all a prank. They were waiting for someone to say, "Surprise. You're on Candid Camera!" Actually, it wasn't a prank. But because the passengers thought it was, they relaxed and had a good time."

So there you have it. Attitudes are more important than facts. All of us have facts about our past. The question is whether or not we allow them to create an attitude of being discouraged. I've never met a non-committed person. One is either committed to remaining where they are or to pushing forward regardless of the challenges. I have a friend in business who went for it and is the most successful man in his field in my area. He said "Yes!" and he's now reaping incredible financial rewards.

Take Nothing for Granted

I'll tell you something else about this top businessman; he won't sit around and listen to a bunch of garbage. He has no time to waste listening to whiny people who lack initiative. He applies the same zeal to his family life as he does to his work. He and his wife live their lives not taking the next day for granted—knowing that today is the time given us to enjoy, care about and help others, and prepare for tomorrow.

Even though my real-life giant bully story at the beginning of this chapter is funny and I love to tell it, there's something we can all learn from it. We may have to face and overcome several giants in our lives in order to get to where we want to be—like David in the Bible. There he was, a kid around 17 years old, getting dressed to take on a giant, Goliath, who was feared by an entire nation. He began putting on Saul's armor; then decided not to wear it after all. He picked up five smooth stones and headed out to meet the Philistine champion. He only needed one stone but Goliath reportedly had four brothers. They met and exchanged angry words. David swung the sling with the smooth stone around and around and then, whoosh! The stone found its intended target and down came that giant, and David eventually became king.

Here's the point I seriously want everyone to get: Some were saying that the giant bully David was facing was too big to hit. David took a good look at him and thought to himself, "He's too big to *miss*!" Wow! That's the way we all need to feel about our dream. Step out and take more control of your life—whatever that means for you. Never live in fear and always remember that your dream is too big for you to miss. Start aiming for it, and watch those success arrows begin hitting the target!

"**I**'ve never met a noncommitted person. One is either committed to remaining where he or she is or to pushing forward regardless of the challenges."

—Jack Smith

"*Passivity based on indecision leads to the demise of many dreams. Action based on positive imagination leads to making them come true.*"

—Jack Smith

—Chapter Sixteen—

Move Out of the Valley of Indecision and Start Climbing Mt. Achievement

*"Indecision keeps us in a
constant state of negative imagination."*
—Jack Smith—

The two sisters, ages 13 and 16, were seated in the same pew they occupied every Sunday with their mother. However, during this worship service, the mother was busy tending to the little ones in the nursery. Sitting in front of the two usually normal teenage kids was a frequent visitor. This woman was always immaculately dressed and very pleasant to be around. She had one characteristic that particularly stuck out, or rather up—her hair was piled high in the once-popular beehive style. Now, when I say high, think *very* high.

The 13-year-old was obviously chewing a big wad of gum— several sticks at once—as the girls rose to sing the song before the sermon. Suddenly, the younger one sneezed and the gum, unknown to the visitor, flew out of the girl's mouth with enough force to sink it into her beehive. The people around them started snickering and pointing. Now what? Should the younger girl tap the lady ever so gently and confess and apologize for what had just happened? Or, would it be best to just leave it alone and let the lady's hair stylist discover the foreign object?

Ask for Help

After the service, the younger sister approached the minister in tears as her indecision was causing her great anxiety. "Preacher, I've done something awful and I need your help to quickly decide what to do," she managed to say between the sobs. She went on to share what had happened, which explained what all the commotion had been about earlier. "Don't look now," she said, "but that's the woman over there." Pointing her out in the crowd, she again asked him to help her decide the best thing to do. "Come with me," he said. "You mean right now?" she asked. "Yes," the preacher said, "she's a visitor and will be gone in a few minutes. We need to act quickly!"

Confront the Situation—*Leave the Valley of Indecision Behind and Start Climbing Mt. Achievement*

The preacher, with the girl walking timidly beside him, approached the unsuspecting visitor and carefully described the situation. By now the young girl was crying so hard, her tears could have watered the flowers at the front of the church! "Young lady, would you please step into the restroom with me so we can talk privately?" the woman asked. The teenager's eyes grew huge, still overflowing with tears, and you could see the sheer terror on her face. With amazing calmness, the visitor gently took the girl by the hand and led her into the ladies' room.

About ten minutes later, they both emerged, smiling, giggling, and seemingly the best of friends. The preacher hardly recognized the lady without her large beehive hairdo which was now tucked under her arm. So, it had been a wig all along! The truth, as she told the girl, was that she had lost her hair due to chemotherapy, and it was just starting to grow back. She said she'd gone so long without hair that when she bought the wig, she wanted a big one to make up for it and get her money's worth!

Many people choose to live in the valley of indecision. They may ask themselves over and over, "Would it be better if I honestly deal with the situation now and get it over with, or just wait and see what happens and maybe it'll go away?" They're so consternated that they just stay stuck. This success-stealing habit carries over to any efforts they may make, perhaps ever so feebly, toward achieving their dreams. Passivity based on indecision leads to the demise of many dreams! As was true in this story, many things in life aren't as challenging as they may first appear, when we might tend to imagine negative outcomes. Blasting through indecision and dealing with the truth in an appropriate way can propel us to our next level of personal development—the one that may be the missing element in making our dream come true. It's not necessarily easy, but such breakthroughs are needed to achieve a new level of success and freedom. Without them, we stay stuck where we are in our thinking. We may even regress and shrink further within the boundaries of the limits we accepted, from ourselves or others.

The Real Versus the Imagined

When talking about success and whomever we've permitted to set our limits, there's the real and the imagined: The gum in the wig was a real situation. What the girl thought the lady would do was a product of her negative imagination. This only reinforced a fearful attitude, spurring her indecisiveness. Her best bet was to have faith that everything would work out just fine—regardless of how the lady chose to respond to her honesty.

A dream is a product of our positive imagination which we need to focus on and mentally amplify. Action based on positive imagination leads to making it come true. However, indecision about a hurdle we need to overcome can keep us in a constant state of negative imagination and unhappiness. As mentioned before, change can be challenging—but it's necessary! Worthwhile endeavors have challenges thrown into the mix. This is normal whenever change is sought.

We can put our foot on the brake or the accelerator. This is first done mentally when we decide what to do—decisively take action or not. Then we physically act on the choice we've made by moving forward or putting on the brakes. One person sees an opportunity, hesitates, and hits the brakes, staying in the land of indecision. Another person sees an opportunity, often the same one, takes full advantage of it, and accelerates on toward his or her goal.

Why?

The answer depends upon many variables: the person's background, psyche, surroundings, supportive family and friends or lack thereof, and, last of all, his or her degree of self-motivating initiative. You know as well as I do that many people aren't self-motivated—they're stuck in negative imagination and the valley of indecision. But at the same time, these people would like things to be better—whether it's financially, spiritually, emotionally, intellectually, or in some other way. If they only had the incentive, knowledge, and support to do so, they'd be more likely to motivate themselves, confront their situations, get on the accelerator, and create a better life.

Are You Accelerating Toward *Your* Goal?

Which one are you doing? Are you stepping on the brakes or putting the pedal to the metal? To get a clearer picture of the analogy, the next time you're in your car, start the engine, put the transmission in drive, and hold the brake pedal down. What happens? Well, there you are in a vehicle that can take you where you want to go but you are choosing to keep the brakes on. Now, put the car in neutral and put your foot on the accelerator. What happens? The engine revs but you don't go anywhere. You have the means to move forward as fast as necessary to reach your destination, but you aren't even in gear. Now, put the transmission in drive and, again, step on the accelerator. What happens? It's called forward motion; you're congruent—your mind, body, and spirit are working together toward accomplishing the goal of this day's journey.

Now listen carefully. We can, just like putting the brakes on or shifting into neutral, make decisions that never get us moving, that keep us stuck. We need to have an encouraging factor—someone or something that will help us reach farther than ever before—to stretch beyond our comfort zone. My encouragement has come from family and friends who gently and kindly nudged me toward doing what I always said I wanted to do. My dream is important to them because I'm genuinely important to them. In fact, even if my dream never came to fruition, they'd love me anyway. How can one not be motivated by a no-lose situation like that?

When *"They"* Don't Think You Can

Yes, but what about those who have family and friends who don't think they can accomplish what they want to do? What if they want to begin a new career, build a business, or do something else, while those who they *think* love and support them say they'll crash and burn?

Let me tell you a story. Once, a solitary squirrel hunter heard something rustling the bushes to his right. Having just a .22-caliber-single-shot rifle, he waited to see what it was, even though he definitely knew it wasn't a squirrel! He thought it may have been a deer, but he wasn't going to shoot at it with a .22, which would have been against the law. His only desire was to see if it was a big buck.

Having Real Motivation

The sound got louder and drew closer. Then it seemed that the entire woods went silent. About 75 yards away, a grizzly bear came crashing into a clearing, running full speed in his direction. He knew what *not* to do, but, in his fright, he did it anyway: He dropped his rifle and ran as fast as he could, away from the on-coming bear—two obvious no noes. With the bear quickly closing in on him, the man ran down a hill into an open meadow with but one lone pine tree growing crookedly in the middle. As he approached it, he quickly noticed that the lowest limb on the tree was at least eight feet off the ground, but he was no high-jumper!

As hopeless as it looked, he had to go for it. With the bear moving in on him, close enough that he could hear his heavy breathing, the hunter reached the tree just ahead of the bear and jumped for his life toward that limb. Well, with his adrenaline pumping, he initially leaped so high that he missed it on the way up, but, thankfully, caught it on the way down. He hung on for dear life until the bear finally realized the man wasn't going to be his lunch. Now that, my friend, is motivation.

Dave Thomas, founder of Wendy's, the third largest hamburger chain in the world, began working at a barbecue restaurant in Knoxville, Kentucky at the ripe old age of 12. Later he met one of the most influential people of his life while moving into management at Kentucky Fried Chicken, Colonel Harland Sanders, founder of KFC. The Colonel was a courageous leader who didn't rest in the valley of indecision.

In 1969, Dave opened his first Wendy's restaurant in Columbus, Ohio. There are now over 6,000 in the United States and Canada, with sales of more than $7 billion. Not bad for a man who started a restaurant he named after his daughter, and decisively acted on his dream. Never one wanting the spotlight, Dave, who was adopted by a Michigan family at six weeks old, would say he was simply a hamburger cook. What an example of a humble man living without limits.

If people tell you it's impossible for you to do something, maybe that's all the motivation you need to get started. Imagine all the fun you'll have proving them wrong! Show them what heights *you* can reach by being 100 percent motivated. Move out of the valley of indecision and start climbing Mt. Achievement. Then encourage your co-workers, family, friends, and associates to do the same.

"**T**his is your life. You can either fulfill your dream or let it die. The choices you make today will help determine how you live tomorrow."

—Jack Smith

"*My* *lack of honesty with myself was my so-called security blanket. I just kept using it for 30 years.... How about you? Are you carrying around a security blan-ket? What are your excuses?*"

—Jack Smith

Chapter Seventeen

What Is Your Security Blanket?

"What's holding you back from living the life you want?"
—Jack Smith—

We may never have met but we have some things in common. Have you ever gone to ride an elevator when the up-arrow button is lit and you push it anyway? So have I. Do we think we have the magic elevator touch? Have you ever gone into a room where the light's on and turned it off thinking you were turning it on? Hello! So have I. We must be related!

The Things We're Likely to Have in Common

Other things many of us have in common are some of the reactions to fears we probably shared in our youth. Did you look under the bed before going to sleep or ask your parents to check in the closets and make sure the windows were locked? Then there was the absolute must when we thought we heard or saw something in the night. We would pull that invincible bulletproof, attack-proof, and fend-off-any-intruder blanket over our heads. We thought that if someone was under the bed or lurking nearby, that person could get us if we left our arms or legs uncovered. What were we thinking?

I was about 10 when I had my first really frightening experience. Friends of my parents were visiting and, as it got closer to my bedtime, Dad told me to brush my teeth and then go to bed. I didn't want to because the hallway leading to my bedroom was long and my room was very dark. But, nonetheless, I walked like a big brave man halfway down the hall, that is, until I was totally out of sight of the grownups. Then I ran into my room, shutting the door behind me, as Dad instructed, so I wouldn't be disturbed by the noise downstairs.

I got out of my clothes, into my pajamas, and in bed with the lights out in record time. Right after I got there, though, I could immediately sense something was wrong. As soon as my eyes adapted to the darkness, I saw a strange man in my room. There he was, silently standing with his back against the closed door to the hallway.

Is There Any Blanket Security?

Frozen with fear, I couldn't say a word. I kept thinking that if I yelled, he'd hurt me, and if I didn't, he may hurt Mom or Dad when they'd come in later to check on me. So I did what most any 10 year-old would do: I pulled the blanket over my head. I'd show him; he couldn't get me if I stayed under the covers!

Breathing hard and fast, but as quietly as I could, I kept waiting for his big move. But as I was peeking out from under the covers, I saw that he was just standing there, still as a statue. I thought about jumping out of the window, but it was dark outside, not to mention a two–story drop to the ground. I finally fell asleep in the wee hours of the morning. When the sun rose so did I. I rubbed my eyes into focus, and he was *still* there! Well, I should say "it" was still there not "him"!

My dear ole' dad had hung his old coat on a nail on the back of the door and placed his hat on top of the coat. It really looked like a big man standing there with his head down as if not wanting to be identified. My mouth couldn't resist its upward thrust into a smile. I got out of bed and got dressed. When I started toward the door, the figure moved toward me. Startled, I jumped back and screamed. However, it was just Dad coming to wake me up. He had opened the door rather quickly, and, to a 10-year-old boy, it looked like the monster had come to life and jumped into an attack mode.

How much security was there in that old blanket? Well, you know as well as I do that there was none except what was imagined in the mind of a young child. So, what security blankets do we use now? Are they really secure?

Justifying What We Do

There are many ways we try to make ourselves right and secure by endeavoring to justify what we do or don't do. When I first moved into a particular town to preach, one of the elderly members of the congregation and his wife invited me to come visit them. He was a great man with a unique sense of humor. Before leaving their home that day, he said he had something to show me. Taking me to his refrigerator, he opened it and pulled out an almost-full bottle of wine.

"Preacher, I know the church frowns on drinking, but I wanted to be up-front with you and let you know that, a while back, I had a problem with my stomach. The doctor prescribed that I drink a glass of wine before going to bed to see if it would help." He then closed the refrigerator door and showed me a yellowed prescription. I couldn't help but notice that the date on it was 1956, and that was in 1978. Jokingly, he said, "Now, preacher, do you see on the prescription anywhere where it says no refills?" His security blanket to justify drinking was a 22-year-old prescription!

An Excuse Maker

I've talked to many people who use supposed security blankets as excuses to never get started at something new. They pull their excuse blankets over their heads like frightened children—thinking that since they can't see anything they must be safe. They justify their actions by making excuses like:

1. I don't have time.
2. I can't do that.

3. That'll never work.
4. I did something like that before.
5. My friends tried it and it didn't work.

Excuses are much the same whether in our faith, business, or other aspects of everyday life. They're just modified to fit the occasion. Excuse makers aren't being honest. Why wouldn't they be forthright and just say they're not interested, if that's the truth? Say "No" firmly and kindly if you're not interested. Just be honest. We want others to be honest with us, rather than stringing us along with excuses. Right? Give others the same courtesy.

A Reformed Security Blanket Carrier

You may be wondering why I suddenly started talking about security blankets. Well, maybe, just maybe, you're like me. I'm a reformed security blanket carrier. No one carried a bigger bag of excuses around than I did. I'm the man who wrote four books and left the manuscripts lying around the office—afraid to let someone read them or send them to a publisher. I'm the one who waited until my 50s to go for the dream I had held inside since my 20s. I was the king of procrastination and used every possible excuse, from dandruff to fallen arches to justify why I never got started.

My lack of honesty with myself was my so-called security blanket. I just kept using it for 30 years, like the man who used the wine prescription for 22. How about you? Are you carrying around a security blanket? What are *your* excuses? This is your life. You can either fulfill your dream or let it die. The choices you make today will determine how you live tomorrow.

"Show others what heights you can reach by being 100 percent motivated. Move out of the valley of indecision and start climbing Mt. Achievement. Then encourage your coworkers, family, friends, and associates to do the same."

—Jack Smith

"You'll be miserable if it's no longer in your heart to do what you're doing for a living. Do something to create a positive change and your life will brighten."

—Jack Smith

—*Chapter Eighteen*—

Are You Listening?

*"I know many people who work at their fulltime jobs, yet day by
day, they're inching toward being financially free."*
—Jack Smith—

It was one of those long nights at the hospital, sitting down beside
the bed of a friend of ours who was in serious condition. I had
only been there for a few hours, while his family had been there
for days. Our friend's wife asked me to step out into the hall so she
could talk to me alone. We were discussing her husband's situation
and the doctor's prognosis, when, all of a sudden, an elderly lady
across the hall started yelling for help.

Later, we were told that this was an every-night occurrence. But
that night the nurses didn't get to her room as quickly as usual. So
the two of us ventured into the woman's room to see what we could
do to help. As soon as we arrived, so did both the doctor and a nurse.
In deference, we stepped back out into the hall but couldn't help
overhearing what was going on inside.

So How's *Your* Hearing?

"How are you this evening?" asked the doctor. "What?" said the
woman, obviously hard of hearing. The doctor repeated what he had
said, but with greater volume, and she responded, "I'm fine; today's
my birthday." "Oh," said the doctor, "are you a Sagittarius?" "What?"

she asked. "I said, are you a Sagittarius?" shouted the doctor. Again she said, "What?" Now getting closer and talking louder he said, "Are you a Sagittarius?" "No," she said, "I'm a Methodist!"

Although that story may sound irrelevant to success, there's something in it that parallels many instances in life. It's similar to when someone who had the knowledge to help cure our woes invested the time to talk frankly to us. We either chose not to listen or didn't understand the person's perspective. There's one obvious difference in the story too. That sweet elderly lady in the hospital had several physical maladies, one of which had apparently left her hearing impaired. The people with the so-called hearing problem to whom I am referring have *no* such maladies. They just simply, as the saying goes, let it go in one ear and out the other.

For example, some people can be told, time and again, how they can reach financial freedom and yet they choose not to listen. They're the same people who complain the loudest about not getting any breaks in life. So, how's *your* hearing?

Missed Opportunities

By age 12, I had collected over 5,000 baseball cards. That year I had at least one card for every player in the American and National leagues. My collection also contained several Babe Ruth, Mickey Mantle, and Willie Mays cards, and on and on. Other kids envied me because of the enormity of my collection. Then came that fateful day when we were to move to another state, and my mother told me she wasn't going to haul a bunch of worthless cards around. I told her that my Little League coach said the cards would be worth a lot some day, and she said that he was simply out of his mind. So I ended up giving all 5,000 cards to a close friend.

There's no telling what they might be worth today, but probably a small fortune. I even started, one time, to look up how much those cards would go for on today's market, got sick to my stomach, and stopped. I can just hear you saying, "Well, all of us have made mistakes like that." That may be true, but it was just one of all too many mistakes for me!

I'm the guy who bought several shares of Wal-Mart stock when it first became available, and then sold it six months later, making a few hundred dollars profit. Unfortunately, after I got rid of it, it split a few times and its value skyrocketed. Had I listened to my broker, who had advised me over and over again to hang onto it, I'd now have over $500,000 in just that one stock!

Learn to Listen to Good Advice

Mark Twain said, "When I was 14, I thought my parents were the dumbest people I had ever known. When I turned 21, I was shocked at how much they had learned in seven short years!" This was, undoubtedly, his way of saying he wished he had listened to them more often.

We have two ears and one mouth. Maybe we need to spend twice as much time listening as talking. This harks back to the wisdom of seeking the advice of those who are already where we want to be. Just passively listening to what they say isn't enough; *hearing* what they say is the key. We need to hear to understand and make the needed application of what we learn, so our life is on the same track that leads to the achievement of our dream.

It may sound like I am implying that it's always easy to do the right things to make our dream a reality. Hey, life-changing activities are seldom easy. Marriage is definitely life-changing but not always easy. How about that first date? Wasn't it both life-changing and awkward, to say the least? That first kiss was strange, too, wasn't it? All were potentially worthwhile, but none were necessarily easy.

Are you listening? You'll be miserable if it's no longer in your heart to do what you're doing for a living. It's no fun to merely exist while going through the motions. Do something to create a positive change and your life will brighten.

Making Tough Decisions

Here's the beauty about going for your goal: You don't have to do it all at once! I know many people who work at their full-time jobs, yet day by day, they're inching toward financial freedom. Once again, let me reiterate that they surround themselves with good people who have high moral standards and integrity. Why is this so important? Because we tend to emulate those we're around the most. Are you still listening? It is said that prominent businessman Ross Perot went so far with this idea that he wouldn't hire anyone who had cheated on his wife. When asked about this, he allegedly said, "If his wife can't trust him, why should I?" Ross Perot didn't become a billionaire without integrity, and you won't fulfill your aspirations without it either. Are you still listening?

"The most successful men and women in history had these two habits in common: They watched what they were doing, always aware of where they were headed. They made course corrections, as needed, to assure that their day by day actions supported their intended destination."

—Jack Smith

—Chapter Nineteen—

Others Are Watching You!

*"If your loved ones and associates or coworkers
duplicated your work ethic, morality, integrity, and goal-reaching,
would you consider them successes?"*
—Jack Smith—

I was a typical 18-year-old kid. One day, Momma, bless her heart, requested that I rake the leaves in the backyard. I asked her why my brother couldn't do it. She said it was because she told me to. I then questioned her, "Why don't you make him help me?" She sternly replied, "I was going to until you got smart with your momma." I knew then that I had better get to the backyard, and quickly!

Grabbing the transistor radio from my room, I ventured to that part of the yard that never looked as huge as it did that day. I remember placing the radio on the outside window ledge, and turning up the volume so I could hear the songs from anywhere in the yard. I then broke into the ridiculous. My attitude was that if I had to do this monumental task, I might as well make it as much fun as possible.

I was prancing and twirling around that backyard like an excited student at his first sock-hop dance. Then one of *those* songs came on the radio. You know what I mean? It's the one that, if you aren't careful, causes you to drive faster. The one that makes you tap your foot. The one that revs you up and makes you feel so good that you do silly things.

Someone's Watching Our Every Move

I stopped raking the leaves and threw my left hand high into the air. Holding the rake handle like a microphone, I began singing with all my heart, along with the radio. Boy was I good! I could even let go of that handle and spin around, catching it before it hit the ground.

I did this for almost the entire song. So why did I stop? It was Momma. I looked up, and there she was, laughing so hard she had to wipe tears from her eyes. This was the day I learned that someone's watching our every move, whether we know it or not.

We All Have Influence

None of us live on this earth without influencing others. We need to determine what type of influence we want to have, and what we're leaving behind to grow for those we love. I'm not just talking about money and things, but a work ethic—stretching for a goal, daring to dream, and the intestinal fortitude to go for it—to be an example for our children and others to follow.

Ask yourself this; and I'll admit, for some, it may be a tough question to answer: If your loved ones and associates or co-workers duplicated your work ethic, morality, integrity, and goal-reaching, would you consider them successes? Others are watching you and learning from what you do. Is what you're doing having a positive or negative impact—especially on those you love, associate, or work with?

How About Doing What We Like to Do?

We're most successful and happy when we're doing what we like to do—to the best of our ability—or bridging to that with a financial vehicle that can free us from doing what we're not now enjoying. Of course, that's contingent on our doing what's morally right and not injurious to ourselves or others. We often accept limits that are stifling to one degree or another. If we're putting all of our efforts toward just paying the bills, what kind of life is that? Wouldn't it be better to live without limits so we can satisfy our longing to be, do, and have what we really want in the long-run.

Others are watching you. So you need to watch yourself too! Every morning, when you look into the mirror, how well do you like the person who's looking back? You *are* watching yourself, aren't you? No one on earth is more familiar with your surroundings, your objectives, and where you want to be than you. No one on earth has more privy to your desires and thoughts than you. It's up to you to live, dream, reach, and stretch, and make sure you don't disappoint yourself.

Where Are We Headed?

If you're a parent, then I probably don't have to tell you about being responsible toward your children. Most parents take that responsibility very seriously, and we all need to so the same in becoming the best we can be. That also means we need to take inventory of our motives and practices. What led us to be where we are at this stage of life? How we can make the necessary changes to establish the life we've been telling ourselves we want?

Momma's no longer with us to look out for my brother and me. But, as we grew, she taught us to never do something just because someone else wanted us to. This could be, of course, different in a job situation. We may need to do things we don't want to do, as long as we're maintaining our integrity, and have agreed, at least temporarily, to accept our employer's compensation. She said, in general, though, if we agree to do something, it needs to be something we really want and deeply desire, or the passion for it will quickly dissipate. By watching out for me, Momma taught me to always watch myself and what I say and do. The most successful men and women today have these two habits in common: They watch what they're doing, and they're always aware of where they're headed. They make course corrections, as needed, to assure their day-by-day actions support their intended destination.

"Look at reaching a certain level in your business as a mountaintop experience. As beautiful and breathtaking as the view is, at one time it was nothing more than a dream. What a beautiful, breathtaking life lies ahead for you—a life of freedom from limits set by others."

—Jack Smith

Chapter Twenty

Treadmill Mentality

*"The world says to go faster, and as long as people
are on the treadmill, they may have been led to believe
they have no other options."*
—Jack Smith—

I have one brother, who I talked about earlier. I'm six-feet-one-inch tall, he's five-feet-six-inches, which will help you understand what I'm about to tell you. Once when he was visiting at our house and I was working out on the treadmill, he asked if he could take a turn on it when I was done. Being the nice guy that I am, I said, "Sure."

It went very smoothly for him at first and he ran for ten minutes. Then, instead of just pushing the red button to stop, he got the not-so-bright idea that he'd hold the side rails and just step off the back. What occurred next happened so fast that, even though I was standing right next to the machine, I couldn't have prevented it.

Getting Off the Treadmill

As his diminutive feet started back and reached the point-of-no-return, he looked straight at me and hollered, "Oh, no!" Then his feet moved faster than I had ever seen before. Like a hamster running in a caged wheel, he stayed upright for a little while. Then the inevitable

happened: Down he went, and in a hurry. I quickly turned the machine off, but not before some damage had been done. Feeling stupid and with his knees skinned, he learned something I was surprised he didn't already know: Never dismount a running treadmill!

For many, daily life is like one long, never-ending treadmill workout, running at full speed. They wake up, reluctant to get on it every morning, five or more days a week, while watching the clock move ever so slowly toward quitting time. They're getting plenty of eye exercise, alright, but they really aren't going anywhere. Their "security" is to never let go of those side rails. Holding on until their knuckles are white is their often-monotonous daily routine. They keep going until someone hits the "stop button." The world says go faster, and as long as the people are on the treadmill, they may have been led to believe they have no other choice. Hopefully, they see someone who got off of it by building a business and bolstered their financial picture. Maybe they'll get it that they can do it too!

The Entrapping Side Rails

The "side rails" offered may be so-called benefits, like security, medical or other insurance, a pension plan, and perhaps occasional raises. Hey, nothing's wrong with that if it's what you really want. But all treadmills have built-in limits. The only one potentially living a rich life while you are on the treadmill is the one who owns it. And some of these owners are basically "owned" by their businesses. They have lots of employees and overhead and aren't any better off in the happiness department, even though they may be financially better off.

So, are you ready to work seriously toward hitting the treadmill stop button and stepping off to pursue your financial freedom? Remember the biblical teaching, "You reap what you sow; you reap more than you sow; and you reap later than you sow." This has a positive and negative side. The positive side is that when we sow properly, we reap a harvest 10-, 20-, or 100-fold. The negative side is best explained by the following example.

There was a farmer who grew the best and most prize-winning watermelons in the area. Early one evening, a young neighbor boy walking down the road, spotted the top of the largest watermelon he'd ever seen, growing right in the middle of the farmer's patch. The boy waited quietly for the cover of darkness. Easing his way stealthily over and around the others, he could finally pick up and break off the stem of that one enormous melon.

Paying the Price

Just as the boy had the huge melon cradled in his arms and was ready to run, the owner of the patch came up behind him, reached out, and grabbed him by the collar. The boy dropped the melon on his own bare foot and you could hear him scream in pain from one end of the county to the other. The farmer pulled the boy roughly through the patch and drove him ten miles to the downtown police station. In a couple days, with disgruntled parents behind him, the boy was standing, foot bandaged and leaning on crutches, in front of the judge who asked how he pled. "Guilty," said the boy. "That will be $15 dollars, son," the judge said with a pound of his gavel. "What? Did you say $15? I don't have $15," the boy protested. Again, the judge repeated the fine. Reluctantly, the boy dug deep into his pocket and paid the fine. It was all the money he had saved from working in the hay fields that summer.

Again, You Reap What You Sow

With a revengeful attitude, the young man who had tried to steal the melon went and gathered all the Johnson's grass seed he could find. This grass gives farmers considerable trouble in growing their crops. Once again, under the cover of darkness, he went into the melon crop owner's field and sowed all the Johnson's grass seed he could. For the rest of his life, that farmer fought the encroachment of the grass. But that isn't the end of the story.

As it turned out, the farmer had a pretty daughter. She and the young man started dating and eventually ended up getting married. When the farmer died, his daughter inherited the farm, and, for the rest of his life, the once-young boy had to fight the Johnson's grass he'd planted years before. What we sow is what we reap!

If we're sowing with a treadmill mentality, then that's as far as we'll go in life in terms of our work satisfaction and financial situation. If we're sowing committed to hitting the stop button once we've achieved an appropriate level of income, then how much more sowing must we do? Establishing a firm financial foundation to be able to later transition into full financial freedom is something that's done over a period of time. Quitting immediately from our present job—the way we pay our bills and support our family—isn't a wise move. We need to be patient as we reach for and gradually create a better life. As wise business mentors say, "Don't quit your day job."

Maybe supplemental income from your own business is exactly what you need to bridge the gap between the treadmill and the financial freedom you yearn for. Building a future where you consistently invest a few additional hours a week outside your job can make a big difference for you financially—as well as help you develop into the person you were meant to be. It is that amount of time when *you* are your own boss and *you* are in charge. What a liberating feeling!

The Mountaintop Experience

Look at reaching a certain level in your business as a mountaintop experience. As beautiful and breathtaking as the view is, at one time it was nothing more than a dream. You will grow it one step at a time and one victory at a time. Then progress will pick up speed as you work with your leader or mentor and leverage with others who are duplicating your committed efforts. What a beautiful, breathtaking life lies ahead for you—a life of freedom from limits set by others.

"Your heartfelt intentions represent a vision of your best life.... Remove the shackles of your limits, and you'll discover you were created to be outstanding."

—Jack Smith

Chapter Twenty One

The Power of Intention

*"Nothing is more important to your future success than
believing in and making your intentions your new reality."*
—Jack Smith—

Imagine a man suffering from agoraphobia—the fear of being in open or public places. After years of special home-visit counseling sessions by the best psychiatrists and thousands of dollars spent, he is ready to step out into the world for the first time in over a decade.

His intention is to go to the shopping mall and just sit for ten minutes. He makes it out the front door and down the porch steps. So far, things are going well. Taking a couple of badly needed deep breaths, he ventures his way down the street.

It's only a four-block journey, and he's already covered two of them. Halfway into the third block, he encounters a man with a large dog. He panics because, in his therapy, he had been trained to be around people, not animals. Fortunately, the man and the dog passed by without incident. Still recuperating from the unexpected appearance of the dog, he stands in one spot, frozen in momentary fear as he now watches a woman pass by holding a cat.

The man turns and runs home as quickly as he can. Bursting through the front door, he yells "I'm safe and never leaving this house again!" He goes into the dining room for some much needed support from his psychiatrist, who is patiently working on his laptop. Much to the man's surprise, a snake is curled up on the psychiatrist's lap!

The moral of the story is that the time and money we've invested to carry out our intentions won't necessarily lead to success, if we haven't done the right things, and therefore, aren't adequately prepared. First of all, this means that we say "Yes!" to our dream. Then we take action on our intention with all our heart, soul, mind, body, and strength, doing whatever's necessary and asking for help as needed. Preparation includes, among other things, participating in continuing education. To fear and not do is to cheat ourselves and compromise the fruition of our intention.

What Are Your Intentions?

Let's face what may be the most important question of all: Since you've decided to live a life without limits, what are your intentions for the future? Speak of them often with people who mentor and support you; write them down and live them. Your heartfelt intentions—based on your dream—represent a vision of your best life.

Borrowing from another familiar quote, "The road to failure is paved with good intentions." What's missing for most people is that they talk a lot about what they wish would happen, but don't take it to the next level by following through with action. Wishes are not intentions. What we intend must be followed up with action, or the intention can never lead to our reality.

What About the Word *"Try"?*

I've preached long enough not to trust that little word "try." If someone tells me he or she will try to attend a class or try to come for counseling, I know that person possesses a halfhearted intention, at best, and won't do it. Did anyone ever tell you he or she would try to come to a meeting or attend a party? It was a no-show, wasn't it?

I've tried to diet and guess what? I still need to lose weight. My intention hasn't been strong enough, even though it seemed like I was motivated. No one would set my limits by telling me it was no use. I found myself succumbing to the idea that my liquid meal replacement tasted really good with a couple scoops of ice cream! I have since focused on this challenge and I can honestly say I'm living the success principles I teach.

Intentions and Lifestyle Improvement

Remove the shackles of your limits, and you'll discover you were created to be outstanding. Step by step, create a healthier, happier, more prosperous lifestyle to help fulfill your intentions. It all ties together. Each element affects the others.

Achieve and maintain optimal health to feel better and have the energy to enhance your lifestyle and fulfill your dream. This involves reprioritizing, just as it does in planning and reaching for a new goal. Anything worthwhile requires effort. The more worthwhile it is the stronger the intention and effort needs to be.

Strong Intentions Fire You Up—*for Action !*

State your intentions. Grab a piece of paper and write them down. Spell them out, then read the list out loud and listen to how it all sounds and feels. Be bold and fearlessly state how you want your life to be. We weren't created with a spirit of fear, but of power and love. Courageously state what you really, really want!

There's a wonderful power found in following through with your intentions. Coming from the depths of the soul, the feeling of accomplishment and peace it gives you is incomparable. Create it for your one precious life, your loved ones, and your legacy. This is the power most people, at some level, want more of in their lives.

Consciously move forward every day toward achieving your intentions—focus on doing what you need to do to make them happen. It's easy to dream about intentions and relatively simple to state them. But it's another story when it comes to implementing them. This is where people who win persist as they continue to take action—even if they don't feel like it. Achieve your intentions by consistently going for what you've stated you want to create for your life—regardless of the odds or obstacles.

You won't find bottled intentions at the store. You can't order them at the pharmacy. The only way you can achieve them is to live each day passionately and resolutely focused on what you're striving for. You doggedly go through the process of following through on your intentions, asking for help as needed from those who have blazed the path before you. There is no other way.

You pull out all the stops and go for it. What do you want to accomplish with the only life you have? If you intend to be the best at something, like building your own business, don't let others talk you out of it by setting limits for you. May their attempt to keep you on the treadmill with them be in vain!

One thing's for sure: We all have a future regardless of how long we may live. What are your intentions now that you have no limits? Nothing is more important to your future success than believing in and making your intentions your new reality. After all, you only have one life to live.

From my perspective as a preacher, I say: What we are is a gift from God. What we become is our gift back to him and his people. What kind of gift are you becoming as you begin *living without limits*?